I0186281

O Allah,

send prayers upon our master Muhammad, the opener of what was closed, and the seal of what had preceded, the helper of the truth by the Truth, and the guide to Your straight path. May Allah send prayers upon his Family according to his grandeur and magnificent rank.

-Salāt al-Fātih

Title: Respecting & Honouring Our Messenger ﷺ

ISBN: 978-1-952306-47-1

FIRST EDITION | JANUARY 2024

Author: Qāḍi ʿIyāḍ b. Mūsa al-Yahsubi
Translator: RASHAD JAMEER
Proofreading: WORDSMITHS
Typesetting: IGP CONSULTING | WWW.IGPCONSULTING.COM
Distribution: WWW.SATTAURPUBLISHING.COM

www.imamghazali.co

Respecting & Honouring Our Messenger ﷺ

Qāḍi ʿIyāḍ b. Mūsa al-Yahsubi

Contents

PUBLISHER'S MESSAGE VII

QĀḌI 'IYĀḌ B. MŪSA AL-YAHSUBI XI

RESPECTING & HONOURING OUR MESSENGER ﷺ

SECTION ONE
ĀYĀT IN THE QUR'AN ON THIS SUBJECT 2

SECTION TWO
ON THE COMPANIONS ﷺ RESPECTING THE PROPHET ﷺ, AND VENERATING HIM AND REVERING HIM 14

SECTION THREE
ON RESPECTING THE PROPHET ﷺ AFTER HIS DEATH, AND WHEN MENTIONING HIM, AND RESPECTING AHL AL-BAYT AND HIS COMPANIONS .. 22

SECTION FOUR
THE SALAF'S RESPECT (*TA'ẒĪM*) FOR THE TRANSMISSION OF THE PROPHET'S HADITHS AND HIS SUNNAH 32

SECTION FIVE
PART OF RESPECTING THE PROPHET ﷺ IS RESPECTING HIS FAMILY, HIS DESCENDANTS, AND HIS WIVES, AS HE ENJOINED AND AS DEMONSTRATED BY THE SALAF AL-ṢĀLIḤ ﷺ 40

SECTION SIX
RESPECT FOR HIS COMPANIONS, DEVOTION TO THEM AND RECOGNIZING WHAT IS DUE TO THEM 54

SECTION SEVEN
THE RESPECT HELD BY THE PROPHET ﷺ FOR HIS POSSESSIONS, FOR HIS LOCALITY IN MECCA AND MEDINA, AND FOR THE PLACES HE VISITED OR ARE WELL-KNOWN BECAUSE OF HIM 66

Publisher's Message

All praise is due to Allah, the First; without a beginning, and the Last; without an end. Peace and prayers be upon the Prophet Muhammad ﷺ, the first Prophet on the Day of Judgement to offer intercession despite being the last Prophet sent, and upon his pure family, his blessed Companions, and all who follow their way upon the path of righteousness, until the day intercession begins with none other than the Prophet Muhammad ﷺ.

Al-Shifā bi Ta'rīf Ḥuqūq al-Muṣṭafā, directly translated as, 'The Remedy (or Cure) Through Recognizing the Rights of the Chosen One', is one of the most celebrated works in the genre of Shamā'il. It stands uniquely amongst the works of Qāḍī 'Iyāḍ as his most celebrated effort–with many surviving manuscripts and commentaries found throughout the Islamic world. Shamā'il is a genre of works that deals with the life, characteristics, and descriptions of the Prophet ﷺ and his station. There are many works in this genre, the most celebrated of which is *al-Shamā'il al-Muḥammadiyyah*, which Imam Ghazali Publishing recently translated and published. Other works include commentaries and summaries of that nature, or hagiographical poems that recount the biography of the Prophet ﷺ and render praise to the Prophetic station.

However, *al-Shifā*, as it is called for short, stands alone as perhaps the most thorough work in this genre, dealing with both the descriptions of the Prophet ﷺ, his station and his perfections, and with the rulings pertaining to one's belief and treatment of him ﷺ. It is exhaustive in its treatment of the subject, expounding on topics that range from Allah's praise of the Prophet ﷺ and his status and station before Him, to the obligation of loving him and what that entails. In short, the uniqueness of this work can be attributed to its holistic coverage of the Messenger ﷺ. Historically, this work took on a form of sacredness and was revered throughout the Muslim world. With that in mind, the Qāḍī's intention for this blessed work was more so to address, what he understood as, a real and practical need in his society. In today's context, it is our intention to continue the spirit of his desire outlined for us in his introduction:

> You have repeatedly asked me to write something which gathers together all that is necessary to acquaint the reader with the true stature of the Prophet, peace and blessings be upon him, with the esteem and respect which is due to him, and with the verdict regarding anyone who does not fulfill what his stature demands or who attempts to denigrate his supreme status—even by as much as a nail-paring. I have been asked to compile what our forebears and imams have said on this subject, and I will amplify it with *ayāt* from the Qur'an and other examples...Writing about this calls for the evaluation of the primary sources, examination of secondary sources, and investigation of the depths and details of the science of what is necessary for the Prophet, what should be attributed to him, and what is forbidden or permissible in respect of him; and deep knowledge of Messenger-ship and Prophethood and of the love, intimate friendship and the special qualities of the sublime rank.[1]

---

1 Iyad ibn Musa, *Muhammad: Messenger of Allah: Ash-Shifā by Qadi 'Iyad* , translated by Aisha Abdarrahman Bewley, vi.

Although it has previously been translated into English in its entirety, our intention with this series is to attempt to bring out, for our readers, some of the most relevant smaller, yet critically important, topics related to the Prophet ﷺ, his station, our duty towards him, and the benefit of loving him and fulfilling our duty towards him. Such a task has been made easier for us by the expert arrangement of the text in terms of its sections and subsections. Each larger section is divided into smaller subsections, which facilitates targeted publications that are small but great in benefit. It is our desire, with having isolated smaller and somewhat easier 'quick-reads', as they are called, that readers may be inspired to complete a full reading of the noble Qāḍī's entire work.

TALUT DAWOOD

IMAM GHAZALI PUBLISHING

—

Qāḍi ʿIyāḍ b. Mūsa al-Yahsubi

The Imām, the unique Ḥāfiẓ, Shaykh al-Islām, ʿAllāmah, Qāḍi Abū al-Faḍl ʿIyāḍ b. Mūsā b. ʿIyāḍ b. ʿUmar b. Mūsā b. ʿIyāḍ al-Yaḥṣubī al-Andalūsi al-Sibti al-Māliki was born in the year 476/1083–84, six months after the Almoravid takeover of the city. His ancestors left Andalus for Fez and then settled in Ceuta. At the age of 22, Qāḍi ʿIyāḍ obtained a license (*ijāzah*) from Ḥāfiẓ Abū ʿAlī al-Ghasāni.

He left Ceuta on two occasions, one of which was to travel to Andalus (Spain) seeking out scholars with whom he could take knowledge. Between 507/1113 and 508/1114 the Qāḍi visited Cordoba, Almeria, Murcia, and Granada. During this time, he learned Ḥadith from the famed scholar, Qāḍi Abū ʿAlī b. Sukrah al-Sadafi. Qāḍi ʿIyāḍ stayed with him closely. He also took Ḥadīth from Abū Baḥr b. al-ʿĀs, Muḥammad b. Ḥamdayn, Abū al-Ḥusayn Sirāj al-Saghīr, Abū Muḥammad b. ʿAttab, Hishām b. Aḥmad and many other scholars. He learned jurisprudence (*fiqh*) from Abū ʿAbdullah Muḥammad b. ʿIsa al-Tamīmī and Qāḍi Muḥammad b. ʿAbdullāh al-Masili.

The Qāḍi was first appointed judge of Ceuta in 515/1121 and served in his position until 531/1136. He would later serve again in Cueta from 539–543/1145–48. His tenure as a judge in Cueta was probably his most productive period; his casework created the foundations for his works in jurisprudence (*fiqh*). Khalaf b. Shakwal said of him:

> He is among the people of knowledge and polymaths, of great intelligence and understanding. He performed the duties of a judge in Ceuta for a long time, in which he earned a praiseworthy reputation. Then he travelled from there for a judgeship in Granada. However, he did not stay there long. Thereafter, he came to us in Cordoba and we took from him.

The jurist (*faqīh*) Muḥammad b. Ḥammadah al-Sibti said:

> The Qāḍi began training at the age of twenty-eight years and assumed judgeship at the age of thirty-five. He was lenient, but not weak, [and] fierce in defence of the truth. He learned jurisprudence (*fiqh*) from Abū 'Abdullah al-Tamīmī and accompanied Abū Isḥāq b. Ja'far. No one in Ceuta wrote more works than him during his time. He wrote the book 'Al-Shifā' fi Sharāf al-Mustafa', 'Tartīb al-Madārik wa Taqrīb al-Masālik fī Dhikr Fuqahā' Madhab Mālik', a multi-volume work, 'Kitāb al-'Aqīdah', 'Kitāb Sharḥ Ḥadīth Umm Zar'', the book 'Jāmi' al-Tārīkh' and others.

Many scholars narrate from Qāḍi 'Iyāḍ. Among them are Imām 'Abdullah b. Muḥammad al-'Ashīri, Abū Ja'far b. al-Qasir al-Gharnāti, al-Ḥāfiẓ Khalaf b. Bashakwal, Abū Muḥammad b. 'Ubayd Allah al-Hijri, Muḥammad b. al-Ḥasan al-Jābirī and his son, Qāḍi Muḥammad b. 'Iyāḍ, the Qāḍi of Denia (in Spain). Qāḍi b. Khalkhan said, 'The teachers of Qāḍi 'Iyāḍ number around one hundred. He passed away during Ramaḍan 544/December-January 1149–50.' Conversely, it has also been reported that he died in Jumada al-Ākhirah of the same year, in Marrakesh. His son passed away in the year 575 AH.

Ibn Bashakwal said, 'Qāḍi 'Iyāḍ passed away to the west of his hometown, in the middle of the year 544 AH." His son, Qāḍi Muḥammad, said, 'He passed away in the middle of the night, on Friday 9 Jumada al-Ākhirah. He was buried in Marrakesh in the year 544 AH.'

al-Dhahabī said, 'it has reached me that he was killed by an arrow for his denial that Ibn Tumart was infallible'.

Some of the Qāḍi's well-known works are:

1. Al-Shifā' bi Ta'rīf Ḥuqūq al-Mustafā – the Shifa' remains one of the most commentated books of Islām.
2. Tartīb al-Madārik wa Taqrīb al-Masālik li Ma'rifat A'lām Madhab Mālik.
3. Ikmāl al-Mu'lim bi Fawa'id Muslim – Qāḍi 'Iyāḍ's own commentary was expounded upon heavily by Imām al-Nawawi in his commentary of Saḥiḥ Muslim.
4. Al-I'lām bi Ḥudūd Qawā'id al-Islām – a work on the five pillars of Islām.
5. Al-Ilma' ilā Ma'rifa Usūl al-Riwāyah wa Taqyīd al-Sama' – a detailed work on the science of Ḥadīth.
6. Mashāriq al-Anwār 'ala Saḥiḥ al-Athar – a work based on the Muwaṭā of Imām Mālik, Saḥiḥ Al-Bukhāri of Imām Bukhāri, and Saḥiḥ Muslim by Imām Muslim.
7. Al-Tanbihāt al-Mustanbaṭah 'ala al-Kutub al-Mudawwanah wa al-Mukhtalaṭah.
8. Daqā'iq al-Akhbar fi Dhikr al-Jannah wa al-Nār – a work describing the joys of Heaven (*Jannah*) and the horrors of Hell (*Jahannam*).

Respecting & Honouring Our Messenger ﷺ

Qāḍi 'Iyāḍ b. Mūsa al-Yahsubi

Exalting the Prophet ﷺ and the Obligation to Respect and Honour Him ﷺ

Section One

FIRST *ĀYAH*

Allah says: "O Prophet! We have sent you as a witness, and a deliverer of good news and a warner." (Aḥzāb 33:45)

SECOND *ĀYAH*

And He says: "so that you believers may have faith in Allah and His Messenger, support (*tu'azzirūhu*) him, honour him, and glorify Allah morning and evening." (Fatḥ 48:9)

THIRD *ĀYAH*

And He says: "O believers! Do not proceed in any matter before a decree from Allah and His Messenger. And fear Allah. Surely Allah is All-Hearing, All-Knowing." (Ḥujurāt 49:1)

FOURTH *ĀYAH*

And He says: "O believers! Do not raise your voices above the voice of the Prophet, nor speak loudly to him as you do to one another lest your deeds become void while you are unaware.

فِي تَعْظِيمِ أَمْرِهِ وَوُجُوبِ تَوْقِيرِهِ وَبِرِّهِ

قال الله تعالىٰ: ﴿يَـٰٓأَيُّهَا ٱلنَّبِيُّ إِنَّآ أَرْسَلْنَـٰكَ شَـٰهِدًا وَمُبَشِّرًا وَنَذِيرًا ﴿٤٥﴾...﴾ الآية [الأحزاب: ٤٥].

﴿لِّتُؤْمِنُوا بِاللَّهِ وَرَسُولِهِ وَتُعَزِّرُوهُ وَتُوَقِّرُوهُ﴾ [الفتح: ٩].

وقال تعالىٰ: ﴿لِّتُؤْمِنُوا۟ بِٱللَّهِ وَرَسُولِهِۦ وَتُعَزِّرُوهُ وَتُوَقِّرُوهُ﴾ [الحُجُرات: ١].

و: ﴿يَـٰٓأَيُّهَا ٱلَّذِينَ ءَامَنُوا۟ لَا تَرْفَعُوٓا۟ أَصْوَٰتَكُمْ فَوْقَ صَوْتِ ٱلنَّبِيِّ وَلَا تَجْهَرُوا۟ لَهُۥ بِٱلْقَوْلِ كَجَهْرِ بَعْضِكُمْ لِبَعْضٍ أَن تَحْبَطَ أَعْمَـٰلُكُمْ وَأَنتُمْ لَا تَشْعُرُونَ ﴿٢﴾ إِنَّ ٱلَّذِينَ يَغُضُّونَ أَصْوَٰتَهُمْ عِندَ رَسُولِ ٱللَّهِ أُو۟لَـٰٓئِكَ ٱلَّذِينَ ٱمْتَحَنَ ٱللَّهُ قُلُوبَهُمْ لِلتَّقْوَىٰ ۚ لَهُم مَّغْفِرَةٌ وَأَجْرٌ عَظِيمٌ ﴿٣﴾ إِنَّ ٱلَّذِينَ يُنَادُونَكَ مِن وَرَآءِ ٱلْحُجُرَٰتِ أَكْثَرُهُمْ لَا يَعْقِلُونَ ﴿٤﴾﴾ [الحجرات: ٢ - ٤].

وقال تعالىٰ: ﴿لَّا تَجْعَلُوا۟ دُعَآءَ ٱلرَّسُولِ بَيْنَكُمْ كَدُعَآءِ بَعْضِكُم بَعْضًا ۚ﴾ [النور: ٦٣].

He says, "Do not make the calling of the Messenger among you like your calling of one another. Indeed, those who lower their voices in the presence of Allah's Messenger are the ones whose hearts Allah has refined for righteousness. They will have forgiveness and a great reward. Indeed, most of those who call out to you, O Prophet, from outside your private quarters have no understanding of manners." (Ḥujurāt 49:2-4)

COMMENTARY ON THE SECOND *ĀYAH*

In the second *āyāh* above: "So that you believers may have faith in Allah and His Messenger, support (*tu'azzirūhu*) him, honour him, and glorify Allah morning and evening." (Fatḥ 48:9), Allah Most High made it an obligation to help (*tu'azzirūhu*) and respect the Prophet ﷺ as well as holding fast to honour and venerate him.

Ibn 'Abbās said: "The word *tu'azzirūhu* means to honour him (*tu-jillūhu*)". Al-Mubarrad said: "*Tu'azzirūhu* means to respect him to the highest degree." Al-Akhfash said: "*Tu'azzirūhu* means to help him gain victory." Al-Ṭabarī said: "*Tu'azzirūhu* means to assist him."

And in another style of Quranic recitation, albeit anomalous (*shādh*), this verse is also recited as *tu'azzizūhu* (honour and strengthen him) as opposed to *tu'azzirūhu* (help him).

COMMENTARY ON THE THIRD *ĀYAH*

In the third *āyāh* above, Allah says: "O believers! Do not proceed in any matter before a decree from Allah and His Messenger. And fear Allah. Surely Allah is All-Hearing, All-Knowing." (Ḥujurāt 49:1), Allah made it forbidden to speak before him; to do so was considered extremely bad behaviour according to Ibn 'Abbās and others. That [opinion] was also preferred by Tha'lab.

فأوجب [اللهُ] تعالىٰ تَعْزِيرَه[1] وَتَوْقِيْرَهُ، وأَلْزَم إكرامَه وتعظيمه.

قال ابن عباس: تُعزِّرُوه: أي تُجِلُّوه. وقال المبرّد: تعزِّروه: تبالغوا في تعظيمه.

وقال الأخفش: تَنْصرونه. وقال الطبري: تُعينونه.

وَقُرِىء[2]: تُعَزِّزُوه - بزايين - من العزّ.

ونُهِيَ عن التقدُّم بين يديْهِ بالقولِ؛ وسُوءِ الأدب بسَبْقِه بالكلام، علىٰ قول ابن عباس وغَيْرِه؛ وهو اختيارُ ثَعْلَبٍ.

قال سَهْلُ بن عبد الله: لا تَقُولوا قبل أَنْ يَقُول؛ وإذا قال فاستمِعُوا له وأَنْصِتوا.

ونُهُوا عن التقدُّم والتعجُّلِ بقَضَاءِ أَمْرٍ قبلَ قَضائِهِ فيه؛ وأَنْ يَفْتَاتُوا بشيء[3] في ذلك مِنْ قِتَالٍ أو غيره من أَمْرِ دِينِهم إلاّ بأمره، ولا يسبقوه به[4]

[و] إلىٰ هذا يرجعُ قولُ الحسن[5]، ومجاهد، والضحّاكِ، والسُّدّي، والثّوري.

ثم وعظَهم وحذَّرهم مخالفةَ ذلك؛ فقال تعالىٰ: ﴿وَٱتَّقُواْ ٱللَّهَۚ إِنَّ ٱللَّهَ

---

(١) في الأصل: «تعزيزه»، والمثبت من المطبوع.

(٢) في الشواذ/ قاله الخفاجي في نسيم الرياض ٣/٣٨٥.

(٣) (أن يفتاتوا): أن ينفردوا ويستبدوا به.

(٤) في الأصل: «ولا يسبقونه به»، والمثبت من المطبوع.

(٥) في المطبوع: «الحسين»: وهو خطأ.

Sahl ibn 'Abdullāh al-Tustarī said: "It means, 'Do not speak before he speaks. When he speaks, listen carefully to him (*istima'*) and be completely silent and attentive (*inṣat*).'"

Moreover, they were forbidden to proceed with and hasten to carry out any matter before he a had made a decision about it. Further, they were forbidden to unilaterally decide any matter in their *dīn* – fighting or otherwise – unless he commanded it. They were not to precede him in this. This is what the statements of al-Ḥasan al-Baṣrī, Mujāhid, al-Dahhāk, al-Suddī and Sufyān al-Thawrī ﷺ say about it.

Allah then warns and cautions them against doing that, concluding the *āyāh* with: "Fear Allah. Allah is All-Hearing, All-Knowing" (49:1).

Al-Mawardī comments on this *āyāh* noting that 'fearing Allah' in this *āyāh* refers to: "Fearing Allah when speaking before the Prophet a speaks, or making decisions before the Prophet decides on a matter."

Al-Sulamī comments on this āyah, saying: "Fear Allah about disregarding what is owed to the Prophet a and neglecting to show him the required respect, because Allah hears what you say and knows what you do."

COMMENTARY ON THE FOURTH *ĀYAH*

In the fourth *āyah*, Allah forbade them to raise their voices above the voice of the Prophet ﷺ or to talk loudly to him a with raised voices in the way that they would talk to each other with raised voices.

It is said: It means do not call Rasūlullāh ﷺ by his name (Muhammad ﷺ) the way that you call each other by your first names.

سَمِيعٌ عَلِيمٌ﴾ [الحجرات: ١] قال الماوَرْديُّ: اتَّقُوا: يعني في التقدُّم.

وقال السُّلَمي: ﴿ٱتَّقُواْ ٱللَّهَ﴾ في إهمالِ حَقِّه وتَضْييع حُرْمَتِه، إنّه سميعٌ لقَوْلكم، عَلِيم بِفعْلكم.

ثم نهاهم عن رَفْعِ الصوتِ فوقَ صَوْتِه، والجَهْرِ له بالقول كما يجْهرُ بعضُهم لبعض ويرفَعُ صوتَه.

وقيل: كما يُنَادِي بعضُهم بَعْضاً باسمه.

قال أبو محمد: مَكّيٌّ: أَيْ لا تُسابِقُوه بالكلام، وتُغْلِظُوا له بالْخِطَاب (١١٩/ب) ولا تُنَادُوه باسْمِه نِداءَ بَعْضِكُمْ لبعض(٦) ولكن عظِّموه ووَقِّروه ونادُوه بأَشرفِ ما يحبُّ أَنْ يُنَادىٰ به: يا رسولَ اللهِ! يا نبيَّ اللهِ!

وهذا كقوله في الآية الأخرىٰ: ﴿لَّا تَجْعَلُواْ دُعَآءَ ٱلرَّسُولِ بَيْنَكُمْ كَدُعَآءِ بَعْضِكُم بَعْضًا﴾ [النور: ٦٣] على أَحَدِ التّأْويلين.

[و] قال غيره: لا تخاطِبوه إلاّ مُسْتَفْهِمين.

ثم خوَّفَهم اللهُ تعالىٰ بحَبْط أعمالهم(٧) إن هم فعلوا ذلكَ، وحذّرهم منه.

١٢٥٠- وقيل: نزلت الآية في وَفْدٍ من(٨) بني تميم - وقيل: في غيرهم؛ أَتَوا النبيَّ ﷺ فنادَوْه: يا محمدُ! يا محمدُ! اخْرُج إلينا. فذمَّهم الله تعالىٰ

---

(٦) في المطبوع: «بعضاً».

(٧) بحبط أعمالهم: أي بطلانها.

(٨) كلمة: «من»، لم ترد في المطبوع.

Abū Muhammad Makkī said: "It means not to speak before him and talk coarsely to him. Do not call him by his name as you do to each other. However, respect and revere him and call him with the noblest title you can use: "*Yā RasūlAllāh* (O Messenger of Allah)" or "*Ya Nabī Allah*" (O Prophet of Allah). This is what Allah says in another *āyah*: "Do not make the calling of the Messenger among you like your calling each other" (Nūr 24:63).

Another scholar said it means: "Do not speak to the Prophet a except when seeking understanding about something."

Then Allah Most High threatened them and frightened them with the cancellation of their deeds if they act that way, cautioning them against it.

1250 – It is said that the *āyāh* was revealed about the delegation of the Banū Tamīm, and others said it was revealed about other people. They came to the Prophet a and called out to him, saying: "O Muhammad! O Muhammad! (*Yā Muhammad! Yā Muhammad!)* Come out to us." Allah reprimanded them for being ignorant and described most of them as being without intellect.

1251 – It is said that the previous *āyāh* was revealed about a conversation between Abū Bakr and 'Umar ﵄ which took place in the presence of the Prophet a. It turned into a dispute and led to them raising their voices.

1252 – It has also been said that it was revealed about Thābit ibn Qays ibn Shammās ﵁, the skillful orator chosen by the Prophet to counter the boasting of Banū Tamīm. Thābit was somewhat deaf and used to raise his voice, so when this *āyāh* was revealed, he stayed in his house, fearing that his good deeds were cancelled. He then went to the Prophet ﷺ and said, "O Prophet of Allah, I fear that I am destroyed. Allah has forbidden us to raise our voices and I am a

بالْجَهْل، ووصفَهم بأَنَّ أكثَرَهم لا يَعْقِلون[٩].

١٢٥١- وقيل: نزلت الآيةُ[١٠] في محاوَرَةٍ كانت بين أَبي بكر وعُمر بين يدي النبيّ ﷺ، واختلافٍ جَرَى بينهما، حتى ارتفعَتْ أَصواتُهما[١١].

١٢٥٢- وقيل: نزلت في ثابت بن قَيْس بن شَمَّاس خَطِيب النبيّ ﷺ في مفاخرة بَنِي تميم، وكان في أُذُنَيْه صَمَم؛ فكان يَرْفَعُ صَوْتَه؛ فلما نزلت هذه الآية أقام في مَنْزِله، وخَشِيَ أَنْ يكونَ حَبِطَ عَملُه؛ ثم أَتَىٰ النبيَّ ﷺ فقال: يا نبيّ اللّٰهِ! لقد خَشيتُ أَنْ أكون هلكتُ؛ نهانا اللّٰهُ أَنْ نَجْهَر بالقَوْلِ، وأنا امرؤٌ جَهِيرُ الصوت.

فقال له النبيُّ ﷺ: «**يا ثابتُ! أَمَا تَرْضَىٰ أَنْ تعيشَ حميداً، وتُقْتَلَ شَهِيداً، وتدخلَ الجنةَ؟** »[١٢] فقُتِلَ يومَ اليمامة[١٣].

١٢٥٣- ورُوي أَنَّ أَبا بكر لما نزلت هذه الآيةُ قال: واللّٰهِ! يا رسولَ اللّٰهِ!

---

(٩) رواه ابن جرير وابن أبي حاتم عن زيد بن أرقم/ مناهل (٩٨٣).

(١٠) في الأصل زيادة: «الأولى».

(١١) أخرجه البخاري (٤٣٦٧) من حديث عبد الله بن الزبير.

(١٢) أخرجه ابن جرير بلفظ المصنف. وأخرجه -بسياقة أخرىٰ- البخاري (٣٦١٣)، ومسلم (١١٩) عن أنس.

(١٣) يوم اليمامة: أي وقعة اليمامة، وكانت المعركة سنة (١٢)هـ في القرية المسماة اليوم بـ «الجبيلة» بقرب «العيينة»، بوادي حنيفة، في نجد، وانتهت المعركة بظفر المسلمين بقيادة خالد بن الوليد، ومقتل مسيلمة الكذاب. ولا تزال إلىٰ اليوم آثار قبور الشهداء من الصحابة، ظاهرة في قرية «الجبيلة» حيث كانت الواقعة، وقد أكل السيل من أطرافها حتى إنَّ الجالس في أسفل الوادي يرىٰ - علىٰ ارتفاع (١٥) متراً تقريباً - داخل القبور ولحدها. انتهى ملخصاً من الأعلام (ترجمة مسيلمة الكذاب).

man with a loud voice." The Prophet ﷺ replied, "O Thābit, are you not content to live in a praiseworthy manner and be killed as a martyr and enter the Garden?" And he was martyred in the Battle of Yamāmah.

1253 – It is related that when this *āyāh* was revealed, Abū Bakr said, "By Allah, O Messenger of Allah, after this I will only speak to you as one speaks when telling a secret!"

1254 – When 'Umar also adopted the manner of speaking like someone telling a secret thereafter, his voice was not audible enough for the Messenger of Allah ﷺ to understand, so Allah revealed this about them: "Those who lower their voices in the presence of the Messenger of Allah are the ones whose hearts Allah has tested for fearfulness. For them is forgiveness and a mighty wage" (Ḥujurāt 49:3).

It is said that the *āyah*: "Those who call unto you from behind the apartments, most of them do not understand" (Ḥujurāt 49:4) was revealed about some other people, not Banū Tamīm, who called the Prophet ﷺ by his first name.

1256 – Ṣafwān ibn 'Assāl related that on one occasion the Prophet ﷺ was on a journey when a Bedouin called out to him in a very loud voice: "Hey Muhammad! Hey Muhammad! (*Ayā Muhammad! Ayā Muhammad!*)." So we told him to lower his voice because we have been forbidden to raise our voices to the Prophet ﷺ. (Tirmidhī 2387)

Allah says: "O you who believe, do not say: '*rā'inā*' (take notice of us)."' (Baqarah 2:104)

One of the Quranic commentators (*mufassirīn*) said that this refers to something in the dialect of the Anṣār which means "take notice of us and then we will take notice of you" but they were forbidden to say

لا أُكَلِّمُكَ بعدها إلا كأخي السِّرَارِ[١٤].

١٢٥٤- وأَنَّ عُمر كان إذا حَدَّثَه حدَّثَه كأخِي السِّرار؛ ما كان يُسمِعُ رسولَ اللهِ ﷺ شيئاً بَعدَ [هذه] الآية حتى يَستَفْهِمَه[١٥].

١٢٥٥- فأَنزل اللهُ [تعالىٰ] فيهم: ﴿إِنَّ ٱلَّذِينَ يَغُضُّونَ أَصْوَٰتَهُمْ عِندَ رَسُولِ ٱللَّهِ أُوْلَٰٓئِكَ ٱلَّذِينَ ٱمْتَحَنَ ٱللَّهُ قُلُوبَهُمْ لِلتَّقْوَىٰ لَهُم مَّغْفِرَةٌ وَأَجْرٌ عَظِيمٌ ۝٣﴾[١٦] [الحجرات: ٣].

وقيل: نزلت: ﴿إِنَّ ٱلَّذِينَ يُنَادُونَكَ مِن وَرَآءِ ٱلْحُجُرَٰتِ....﴾ [الحجرات: ٤] في غير بني تميم؛ نادَوه باسْمِه.

١٢٥٦- ورَوَىٰ صَفْوانُ بن عَسَّال: بَيْنَا النبيُّ ﷺ في سَفر إذ ناداهُ أَعرابيٌّ بصوتٍ له جَهْوَري: أَيَا محمدُ! أَيَا محمدُ! فقلنا له: اغْضُضْ من صَوْتِك؛ فإنكَ قد نُهِيتَ عن رَفْعِ الصوت[١٧].

---

(١٤) أخرجه البزار ٦٩/٣ برقم (٢٢٥٧) من حديث أبي بكر، وصححه الحاكم (٧٤/٣)، وردَّه الذهبي بقوله: «حصينٌ واهٍ». وقال الهيثمي في المجمع ١٠٨/٧: «فيه حصين بن عَمْرٍو الأحمسي، وهو متروك، وقد وثقه العِجْليُّ، وبقية رجاله رجال الصحيح». وقال ابن كثير في التفسير ٢٠٦/٤: «حصين بن عمرو، هذا، وإنْ كان ضعيفاً، لكن قد رويناه من حديث عبد الرحمن بن عوف، وأبي هريرة رضي الله عنهما بنحو ذلك، والله اعلم». (كأخي السِّرار) السِّرار: المُسارَرة: أي كصاحب السِّرار، أو كَمِثْل المُسارَرَةِ، لخفض صوته، والكاف صفة لمصدر محذوف/ النهاية.

(١٥) أخرجه البخاري (٧٣٠٢)، وهو طرف من الحديث المتقدم برقم (١٢٥١). (لا يسمعه حتى يستفهمه) تأكيد لمعنى قوله: «كأخي السِّرار» أي: يخفض صوته، ويبالغ، حتى يحتاج إلى استفهامه عن بعض كلامه/ الفتح ٢٨٠/١٣.

(١٦) رواه ابن جرير، المناهل (٩٨٨).

(١٧) أخرجه الترمذي (٢٣٨٧)، والنسائي في التفسير في الكبرىٰ. وقال الترمذي: «هذا حديث حسن صحيح».

out of respect (*ta'ẓīm*) for the Prophet. They were forbidden to say it since it has the implication and insinuation of: "they will only take notice of him if he takes notice of them first." But rather, it is the right of the Prophet ﷺ that we must take notice of him in any situation.

It is said that the Jews used to say "*rā'inā*" in order to mock the Prophet ﷺ.[1] Muslims were subsequently forbidden to say this in order to prevent this insult from occurring, and also not to resemble the Jews through the use of a similar phrase that they were using. Other things have been said as well.

---

1 Translator's Note: The word *rā'ī* means shepherd in Arabic, and a shepherd gives care to his flock and pays attention to them all, so when the Companions ﷺ were saying: "*rā'inā*", they were saying: "Pay attention to us" out of love and affection for the Prophet ﷺ. But when the vile Jews used to say "*rā'inā*" to the Prophet ﷺ, they were saying: "Our little shepherd boy". May Allah's wrath be upon them!

وقال الله تعالىٰ: ﴿يَـٰٓأَيُّهَا ٱلَّذِينَ ءَامَنُواْ لَا تَقُولُواْ رَٰعِنَا...﴾ [البقرة: ١٠٤].

قال بعض المفسرين: هي لغةٌ كانت في الأنصارِ؛ نُهُوا عن قَوْلها تعظيماً للنبيِّ ﷺ، وتَبْجيلاً له؛ لأنَّ معناها: ارْعَنا نَرْعَكَ [فَنُهُواعن قَوْلها؛ إذْ مُقْتضاها، كأنهم لا يرعَونَه إلاَّ بِرعايتهِ لهم؛ بل حقُّه أَنْ يُرْعَىٰ] علىٰ كلِّ حال.

وقيل: كانت اليهودُ تُعرِّضُ [بها] للنبيِّ ﷺ بالرُّعونة؛ فَنُهِي المسلمون عن قَوْلها؛ قَطْعاً للذَّرِيعة، ومَنْعاً للتَّشبيه بهم في قولها، لمشاركة اللفظ. وقيل غَيْرُ هذا.

(جَهْوَريّ): شديدٍ عالٍ/ النهاية.

Section Two

On the Companions ﷺ Respecting the Prophet ﷺ, and Venerating Him and Revering Him

1257 – 'Amr ibn al- 'Āṣ ﷺ said: "There is no one more beloved to me than the Messenger of Allah a, nor is anyone more respected in my eyes than he. I was never able to bring myself to stare at him a for the least amount of time because of my immense respect (*ijlāl*) for him. If I had been asked to describe him, I could not have done so because I was unable to look at him [for long] enough." (Muslim 121)

1258 – Al-Tirmidhī records that Anas ﷺ said: "The Messenger of Allah ﷺ used to come out to his Companions among the Muhājirīn and Anṣār while they were sitting down, and Abū Bakr and 'Umar ﷺ were also among them. None of them would raise their eyes to look directly at him except Abū Bakr and 'Umar. Those two would look at him a and he would look at them, and they would smile at him and he would smile at them." (Tirmidhī 3668)

1259 – It is related that Usāmah ibn Sharīk ﷺ said: "I came to the Prophet ﷺ and found his Companions sitting around him so still and motionless as if there were birds on their heads." (Abū Dāwūd 3855)

فصل

فِيْ عَادَةِ الصَّحَابَةِ فِيْ تَعْظِيْمِهِ عَلَيْهِ السَّلامُ وَإِجْلالِهِ وَتَوْقِيْرِهِ

١٢٥٧- حدثنا القاضي أَبو علي الصَّدَفي، وأبو بَحْرٍ الأَسَدِي بسماعي عليهما في آخرين؛ قالوا: حدثنا أَحمد بن عُمَر، حدثنا أحمدُ بن الْحَسَن، حدثنا محمد بن عيسىٰ، حدثنا إبراهيم بن سُفْيان، حدثنا مُسْلم، حدثنا محمد بن المُثَنّىٰ، وأبو مَعْن الرَّقَاشي، وإسحاق بن منصور؛ قالوا: حدثنا الضحّاك بن مَخْلَد، حدثنا حَيْوَةُ بن شُرَيح، حدثني يزيد بن أبي حَبيب، عن ابن شُمَاسَة المَهْرِيّ؛ قال: حَضَرْنَا عَمْرَو بنَ العاص...فذكر حديثاً طَوِيلاً فيه عن عَمْرو، قال: وما كان أحدٌ أَحبَّ إليَّ مِنْ رسولِ الله ﷺ، ولا أَجَلَّ في عَيْني منه، وما كنتُ أُطيقُ أَنْ أملأَ عَيْنَيَّ منه إجلالاً له؛ ولو سُئلتُ أَنْ أَصِفَه ما أطقتُ؛ لأَني لم أَكُنْ أملأُ عَيْنَيَّ منه.

١٢٥٨- ورَوَى التِّرمذي، عن أَنس، أَنَّ رسولَ الله ﷺ كان يخرجُ علىٰ أَصحابه من المُهَاجرين والأنصار وهم جلوسٌ، فيهم أبو بكر، وعُمر؛ فلا يرفَعُ أَحدٌ منهم بَصَرَه إليه إلاَّ أبو بكر وعُمرُ؛ فإنهما كانا ينظُرَانِ

1260 – In a hadith describing the Prophet ﷺ, we find: "…when he spoke, those sitting around him bowed their heads (out of respect for him) as if there were birds on their heads."

1261 – When Quraysh sent 'Urwah ibn Mas'ūd ؓ to the Messenger of Allah a in the year of the Treaty of al-Hudaybiyyah, 'Urwah said that he had never seen the level of respect (*ta'ẓīm*) that the Companions were showing to Rasūlullāh a. Whenever he did *wuḍū'*, they rushed to gather his leftover *wuḍū'* water and were almost fighting over it. If he spat, or cleared his throat then spit, they took it with their hands and wiped it on their faces and bodies. If a single hair of his a fell off, they rushed to collect it. If he commanded them to do something, they ran to fulfill his command. If he spoke, they lowered their voices in his presence. They did not directly stare at him due to their respect (*ta'ẓīm*) for him.

When 'Urwah ؓ returned to Quraysh, he said: "O People of Quraysh! I have visited Chosroes (the Persian King) in his kingdom, Caesar (the Roman King) in his kingdom, and the Negus (the African King) in his kingdom, but I swear by Allah, I have never seen any king among his people treated the way Muhammad is treated by his Companions." (Bukhārī 2731-2732)

Another narration has it: "I have never seen a king whose companions respect him (*ta'ẓīm*) as much as Muhammad is respected by his Companions. I have seen a people who will *never* abandon him."

1262 – Anas ؓ said: "I saw the Messenger of Allah ﷺ when the hair on his head was being shaved. His Companions ؓ were going around him, and they did not want his hair to fall after being cut, except into the hand of a man [i.e. not onto the ground! What love!]." (Muslim 2325)

إليه وينظر إليهما، ويتَبَسَّمان إليه، ويبتسَّمُ إليهما.

١٢٥٩- ورَوَىٰ أُسامةُ بن شَرِيك؛ قال: أَتيت النبيَّ ﷺ وأصحابُه حولَه كأنما علىٰ رُؤُوسِهم الطَّيْرُ[١٨].

١٢٦٠- وفي حديث صِفَتِه: إذا تكلَّم أَطرق جلساؤه[١٩] كأنما علىٰ رُؤوسهم الطير[٢٠].

١٢٦١- وقال عُروة بن مسعود حين وجَّهَتْه قُرَيش عامَ القضيّة[٢١] إلىٰ رسُولِ الله ﷺ، فرأى من تعظيم أصحابه له (١٢٠/ب) ما رأى، وأنه لا يتوضّأ إلا ابتَدَرُوا وَضُوءه، وكادوا يَقْتَتِلون عليه، ولا يَبْصُق بُصاقاً، ولا يتنخَّمُ نُخَامَةً إلا تلَقَّوْها بأكفِّهم فدَلكُوا بها وُجوهَهم وأجسادَهم؛ ولا تسقُط منه شعرةٌ إلاَّ ابْتَدَرُوها؛ وإذا أمرهم بأَمْرٍ ابْتَدَروا أَمْرَه؛ وإذا تكلَّم خَفَضُوا أصواتَهم عنده، وما يُحِدُّون إليه النظَر تعظيماً له. فلما رجعَ إلىٰ قُريش، قال: يا مَعْشَر قُريش! إني جئْتُ كِسْرَىٰ في مُلْكه، وقَيْصَرَ في مُلْكه، والنَّجَاشي[٢٢] في مُلكه؛ وإني، واللهِ! ما رأَيْتُ مَلِكاً في قومٍ قَطُّ مثل

---

(١٨) أخرجه أبو داود (٣٨٥٥) وغيره. وصححه أكثر من واحد. وقد استوفينا تخريجه في موارد الظمآن (١٣٩٥). (كأنما علىٰ رؤوسهم الطير): وصَفَهم بالسكون والوقار، وأنهم لم يكن فيهم طيش ولا خفة، لأن الطير لا تكاد تقع إلا على شيء ساكن/ النهاية.

(١٩) في الأصل: «أطرقوا كلهم»، والمثبت من المطبوع ومن مصادر تخريج الحديث.

(٢٠) فقرة من حديث الحسين بن علي عن أبيه المتقدم برقم (١/٣٧٤). (أطرق): أمال رأسه إلىٰ صدره وسكت فلم يتكلم/ المعجم الوسيط.

(٢١) عام القضية: أي عام صلح الحديبية سنة ست من الهجرة.

(٢٢) في الأصل: «والنجاشي رحمه الله».

1263 – Another instance of this is when Quraysh gave 'Uthmān ﷺ permission to perform *ṭawāf* (circumambulation) of the Kaaba when the Prophet ﷺ sent him as an envoy to them, but he refused, saying: "I will not do ṭawāf until the Messenger of Allah a does ṭawāf first." (Bayhaqī)

Note: The next hadith is referring to the *āyah* of Qur'an: "Among the men are those who were true to their covenant with Allah, some of them have fulfilled their vow by death and some of them are still waiting." (Aḥzāb 33:23)

1264 – Ṭalḥah ibn 'Ubaydillāh ﷺ said that the Companions of the Messenger of Allah ﷺ requested an unlearned Bedouin: "Ask the Prophet ﷺ about what is meant by someone who has 'fulfilled his vow.'" They asked the Bedouin to do so because they held such a high level of awe and respect for the Prophet ﷺ. He asked the Prophet ﷺ but he did not respond. Then when Ṭalḥah ﷺ approached the Messenger of Allah, the Prophet said: "This is someone who has fulfilled his vow."[2] (Tirmidhī 3742)

1265 – Qaylah ﷺ said: "When I saw the Messenger of Allah a sitting in a squatting position, I trembled from fear." This was out of her awe and respect (*ta'ẓīm*) for him.

1266 – Al-Mughīrah ﷺ said: "The Companions of the Messenger of Allah a would knock on his door with their fingernails [out of respect for him]." (Al-Ḥākim and al-Bayhaqi)

---

2 Translator's Note: That is because Ṭalḥah ibn 'Ubaydillāh ﷺ stayed firm when he met the enemy on the battlefield during the battle of Uḥud and did not flee. In fact, he was jumping in front of arrows in order to protect the Prophet ﷺ from being hit by them. (Jāmi' al-Usūl 5/9) He had 70 scars on his body after that battle, and one of his hands was left paralyzed for the rest of his life due to him blocking arrows from hitting the Prophet ﷺ using his body.

محمدٍ في أصْحَابه[٢٣]. وفي رواية: إنْ رأيتُ مَلِكاً قطُّ يُعظّمه[٢٤] أصحابُه ما يُعَظِّمُ محمداً أصحابُه. وقد رأيتُ قوماً لا يُسْلِمُونه أَبداً.

١٢٦٢- وعن أنس: لقد رأيتُ رسولَ الله ﷺ والحلاَّق يحلقُه، وقد أطاف به أصحابُه، فما يُريدون أن تَقَع شعرةٌ إلاَّ في يَدِ رَجُل.

١٢٦٣- ومن هذا لمّا أذِنَتْ قُريش لعُثمانَ في الطَّواف بالبيت حين وجَّهه النبيُّ ﷺ إليهم في القَضِيَّة أَبَى، وقال: ما كُنْتُ لأَفْعَلَ حتى يطوفَ به رسولُ الله ﷺ.

١٢٦٤- وفي حديث طَلْحَةَ: إنَّ أصحابَ رسولِ الله ﷺ قالُوا لأَعرابي جاهلٍ: سَلْهُ عمَّنْ قَضَىٰ نَحْبَهُ - وكانوا يَهَابونَه ويوقّرونه - فسأله، فأَعرض عنه، إذ طلع طَلْحةُ، فقال رسول الله ﷺ: «**هذا مِمَّنْ قَضَى نَحْبَهُ**».

١٢٦٥- وفي حديث قَيْلَةَ: فلما رأيتُ رسول الله ﷺ جالساً القُرْفُصاءَ أُرْعِدْتُ من الفَرَق. وذلك هَيْبَةً له وتعظيماً.

١٢٦٦- و في حديث المغيرة: كان أصحابُ رسولِ الله ﷺ يقْرَعُون بابَهُ بالأظافير[٢٥].

---

(٢٣) أخرجه البخاري (٢٧٣١، ٢٧٣٢) من حديث المِسْوَرِ بن مَخْرَمة ومروان بن الحكم. (ابتدروا وَضوءه): أي أسرعوا إلىٰ الماء الذي توضَّأ به ليأخذوه تبركاً. (النخامة): ما يلفظه الإنسانُ من البلغم/ المعجم الوسيط. (ما يُحِدُّون): أي ما يديمون/ الفتح ٣٤١/٥.

(٢٤) في الأصل زيادة: «مِن».

(٢٥) أخرجه الحاكم في معرفة علوم الحديث ص: (١٩)، والبيهقي في المدخل كما في المناهل (٩٩٨). وفي

1267 – Al-Bara' ibn 'Azib ؓ said, "I wanted to ask the Messenger of Allah a about something but waited for years to do so out of awe of him." (Abū Ya'lā)

١٢٦٧-[و] قال البَراء بن عازب: لقد كنتُ أُرِيدُ أن أَسأَل رسولَ الله صلى الله عليه وسلم عن الأمر فأؤخّره سِنين مِنْ هَيْبَتِهِ[٢٦].

الباب: عن أنس بن مالك عند البزار (٢٠٠٨)، قال الهيثمي في المجمع (٤٣/٨): «وفيه ضرار بن صرد، وهو ضعيف»، ورمز لضعفه أيضاً السيوطي في الجامع الصغير (٦٨٢٧) وانظر فيض القدير ١٦٩/٥. (يقرعون بابه بالأظافير) أي: يطرقون بأطراف أظافر الأصابع طرقاً خفيفاً، بحيث لا يزعج، تأدباً معه، ومهابة له.

(٢٦) رواه أبو يعلى الموصلي/ المناهل (٩٩٩). ولم أجده في المسند الذي حققه أستاذنا الفاضل حسين أسد. ولعله في مسنده الكبير برواية ابن المقرىء.

Section Three

On Respecting the Prophet ﷺ After His Death, and When Mentioning Him, and Respecting Ahl al-Bayt and His Companions

Know that upholding the sacredness and holiness (*ḥurmah*) of the Prophet ﷺ after his death, and respecting him and venerating him, is obligatory in the same manner that it was obligatory when he was alive ﷺ. In other words, [follow the same commandements] whenever he is mentioned ﷺ, or his hadith or Sunnah are mentioned, or when anyone hears his name or anything about his life, or how his family and relatives (*'itrah*) behaved, or respecting his Ahl al-Bayt (Household) and his Companions.

Abū Ibrāhīm al-Tujībī said: "It is obligatory (*wājib*) for every believer – when he mentions the Prophet ﷺ or the Prophet is mentioned to him – to be humble, reverent, respectful, and to be still and motionless, not moving too much. He should be as respectful and dignified as he would be if he were actually in the holy presence of the Prophet ﷺ, and he should display the *adab* (manners) which Allah taught us to show him ﷺ."

Qāḍī Abū'l-Faḍl said: "This is the way our Pious Predecessors (the *Salaf*) and Great Imams behaved ﷺ."

1268 –Abū Humayd said: "Abū Ja'far, the *Amīr al-Mu'minīn* (Commander of the Believers) of that time, had a dispute with Imam Mā-

فصل

[فِيْ تَعْظِيمِ النَّبِيِّ ﷺ بَعْدَ مَوْتِهِ، وَعِنْدَ ذِكْرِهِ، وَتَعْظِيمِ أَهْلِ بَيْتِهِ وَصَحَابَتِهِ][٢٧]

واعلم أنَّ حُرمَةَ النبيِّ ﷺ بعد موتِه، وتوقِيرَه وتعظيمَه، لازمٌ كما كان في حال حياتِه؛ وذلك عند ذِكرِه - عليه السلام - وذِكرِ حديثه وسُنَّتِه، وسَمَاعِ اسْمِهِ وسيرته، ومُعَاملةِ آلِهِ وعِتْرَته[٢٨]، وتعظيم أهل بيته وصحابته. وقال أبو إبراهيم: إسحاق التُّجِيبي[٢٩]: واجبٌ (١٢١/أ) على كل مُؤمنٍ متى ذَكرَه - أو ذُكِر عنده - أنْ يخضَعَ ويَخْشع، ويتوَقَّر ويسكنَ مِنْ حركته، ويأخُذَ في هَيْبَتِه وإجلالِه بما كان يأخُذ به نَفْسَهُ لو كان بين يَدَيْه؛ ويتأَدَّبَ بما أَدَّبَنَا[٣٠] اللهُ به. قال القاضي أبو الفضل: وهذه كانت سيرةَ سَلَفِنَا الصالِح وأَئمتنا الماضين رضي الله عنهم أجمعين.

---

(٢٧) ما بين حاصرتين من عندي.

(٢٨) وعترته: عِتْرة النبي ﷺ: بنو عبد المطلب. وقيل: أهل بيته الأقربون، وهم أولاده وعليٌّ وأولاده. وقيل: عترته: الأقربون والأبعدون منهم/ النهاية.

(٢٩) في الأصل: «قال أبو إسحاق إبراهيم التجيبي»، والمثبت من سير أعلام النبلاء ٧٩/١٦.

(٣٠) في الأصل: «أدبه»، والمثبت من المطبوع.

lik in the Prophet's masjid a, and Imam Mālik said to him: 'O 'Amīr al-Mu'minīn, do not raise your voice in this masjid, because truly Allah taught people the *adab* (manners) of being here by saying: "O believers! Do not raise your voices above the voice of the Prophet, nor speak loudly to him as you do to one another or your deeds will become void while you are unaware" (Ḥujurāt 49:2).

And He praised people by saying: "Indeed, those who lower their voices in the presence of Allah's Messenger are the ones whose hearts Allah has refined for righteousness. They will have forgiveness and a great reward" (Ḥujurāt 49:3).

And He rebukes people, saying: "Indeed, most of those who call out to you O Prophet from outside your private quarters have no understanding of manners" (Ḥujurāt 49:4). And truly, the sacredness (*ḥurmah*) of the Prophet ﷺ after his passing is the exact same as his sacredness was when he was alive.

"Abū Ja'far was humbled by this, and asked Imam Mālik: 'O 'Abū 'Abdullāh, should I face the *qiblah* when I make *du'ā*, or face the Messenger of Allah a and make *du'ā*?' He replied: 'Why would you turn your face away from him when he is your means and the means of your father, Adam, to reach Allah on the Day of Judgement? Rather, I turn my face to him a and ask him directly to intercede for me, and Allah will grant his intercession. Allah says: "We only sent messengers to be obeyed by Allah's Will. If only those hypocrites came to you O Prophet – after wronging themselves – seeking Allah's forgiveness and the Messenger prayed for their forgiveness, they would have certainly found Allah ever Accepting of Repentance, Most Merciful."(Nisā' 4:64). (Imam al-Khafajī has authenticated its chain in Nasīm al-Riyāḍ 3/398)

١٢٦٨- حدثنا القاضي أبو عبد الله: محمد بن عبد الرحمن الأَشعري، وأبو القاسم: أحمد ابن بَقِيّ الحاكم، وغيرُ واحد، فيما أجازُونيه؛ قالوا: حدثنا أبو العباسِ: أحمد بن عمر بن دِلْهاث [قال] حدثنا أبو الحسن: على بن فهر، حدثنا أبو بكر[٣١]: محمد بن أحمد بن الفَرَج، حدثنا أبو الحَسَن: عبد الله بن المُنْتَاب، حدثنا يعقوب بن إسحاق ابن أبي إسرائيل، حدثنا ابنُ حُمَيْد؛ قال: ناظرَ أَبو جَعْفرٍ أميرُ المؤمنين مَالِكاً في مسجدِ رسولِ الله ﷺ، فقال له مَالِكٌ: يا أمير المؤمنين! لا ترفع صَوْتَك في هذا المسجد، فإن الله عَزَّوَجَلَّ أَدَّبَ قوماً فقال: ﴿لَا تَرۡفَعُوٓاْ أَصۡوَٰتَكُمۡ فَوۡقَ صَوۡتِ ٱلنَّبِيِّ وَلَا تَجۡهَرُواْ لَهُۥ بِٱلۡقَوۡلِ كَجَهۡرِ بَعۡضِكُمۡ لِبَعۡضٍ أَن تَحۡبَطَ أَعۡمَٰلُكُمۡ وَأَنتُمۡ لَا تَشۡعُرُونَ﴾ [الحجرات: ٢]. ومدَح قوماً فقال: ﴿إِنَّ ٱلَّذِينَ يَغُضُّونَ أَصۡوَٰتَهُمۡ عِندَ رَسُولِ ٱللَّهِ أُوْلَٰٓئِكَ ٱلَّذِينَ ٱمۡتَحَنَ ٱللَّهُ قُلُوبَهُمۡ لِلتَّقۡوَىٰۚ لَهُم مَّغۡفِرَةٞ وَأَجۡرٌ عَظِيمٌ﴾ [الحجرات: ٣].

وذمَّ قوماً فقال: ﴿إِنَّ ٱلَّذِينَ يُنَادُونَكَ مِن وَرَآءِ ٱلۡحُجُرَٰتِ أَكۡثَرُهُمۡ لَا يَعۡقِلُونَ﴾ [الحجرات: ٤] وإِنَّ حُرۡمَتَه ميتاً كحُرۡمَتِه حيّاً.

فاستكان لها أبو جَعْفرٍ[٣٢]، وقال: يا أبا عبد الله! أَأَسْتَقْبِلُ القِبْلَةَ وأَدْعُوا أم أستقبلُ رسولَ الله ﷺ وأدعو؟ فقال: ولِمَ تصرفُ وجْهَك عنه وهو

---

(٣١) في الأصل زيادة: «بن» والمثبت من المطبوع.

(٣٢) أي خضع وخشع وذلّ.

When Imam Mālik was asked about Sheikh Ayyūb al-Sakhtiyānī, he said: "I have not reported from anyone except that Ayyūb is better than him." He went on saying: "I performed hajj twice and watched him, but did not listen to his talks. Then one day I saw that when the Prophet ﷺ was mentioned, he wept so much that I had to console him. When I saw what I saw from him, and the immense respect he had for the Prophet ﷺ, from that moment on I began writing things down from him."

Muṣ'ab ibn 'Abdullāh (whose fifth grandfather is Zubayr ibn al-'awwām ؓ) said: "When the Prophet ﷺ was mentioned, Imam Mālik would turn pale to the point that it distressed those sitting with him. One day he was asked about it, and he said: 'If you had seen what I have seen, you would not be surprised at what you see happen to me. I used to see Muhammad ibn Munkadir – the master of the Qur'an reciters – almost every single time he was asked about a hadith. He wept so much until we had to console him.'"

Muṣ'ab ibn 'Abdullāh[3] said:

"I saw Imam Ja'far al-Ṣādiq ؓ – who usually had a jovial personality, a good sense of humour, and smiled a lot – when the Prophet ﷺ was mentioned in his presence, and he turned pale. And I never saw him relate a hadith of the Messenger of Allah ﷺ except in a state of purity (*ṭahārah*).

I visited him frequently for quite some time, and I only saw him doing one of three things: praying salat, fasting, or reciting Qur'an. He did not speak about things that did not concern him. He was one of the scholars and worshippers who truly feared Allah Most High.

---

3 Translator's Note: Imam Mālik may have also said this.

وَسِيلتُك وَوَسِيلةُ أبِيكَ آدمَ -عَلَيْهِ السَّلَامُ- إلىٰ الله [تعالىٰ] يوم القيامة؟ بل استقبلْهُ واستَشْفِعْ بهِ، فيشفِّعه(٣٣) اللهُ؛ قال الله تعالىٰ: ﴿وَلَوْ أَنَّهُمْ إِذ ظَّلَمُوٓاْ أَنفُسَهُمْ جَآءُوكَ فَٱسْتَغْفَرُواْ ٱللَّهَ وَٱسْتَغْفَرَ لَهُمُ ٱلرَّسُولُ لَوَجَدُواْ ٱللَّهَ تَوَّابًا رَّحِيمًا﴾ [النساء: ٦٤].

وقال مالك - وقد سُئِل عن أيوب السَّخْتِياني-: إني ما حدثتُكم عن أَحدٍ إلا وأيوب أَفضل منه. قال: وحَجَّ حِجَّتَيْن، فكنْتُ أَرْمُقُهُ ولا أسمَعُ منه، غير أنه كان إذا ذُكِرَ النبيُّ ﷺ بكىٰ حتى أَرْحَمَهُ! فلما رأيتُ منه ما رأيتُ، وإجلالَه للنبي ﷺ كَتَبْتُ عنه. وقال مُصْعَب بن عبد الله: كان مالك إذا ذُكر النبيُّ ﷺ يتغيَّر لونُه (١٢١/ب)، ويَنْحَني حتى يَصْعُبَ ذلك علىٰ جُلسائه؛ فقيل له يوماً في ذلك، فقال: لو رأيتُم ما رأيت لما أنكرتُم عليّ ما تَرَوْن؛ ولقد كنت أرىٰ محمد بن المُنْكَدِر(٣٤) -وكان سيّدَ القُرّاء- لا يكادُ يسألُه أحدٌ عن حديثٍ(٣٥) أبداً إلاَّ يَبْكي حتى نَرْحَمَه.

ولقد كنتُ أَرَىٰ جعفَر بن محمد الصادق، وكان كثيرَ الدُّعَابةِ والتبسُّم؛ فإذا ذُكر عنده النبيُّ ﷺ اصْفَرَّ. وما رأَيتُه يحدِّثُ عن رسولِ الله ﷺ إلا علىٰ طَهارةٍ.

---

(٣٣) في المطبوع: «فيشفعك».

(٣٤) إمام حافظ قدوة، كان من سادات القُرّاء. ولد سنة بضع وثلاثين للهجرة. ومات سنة (١٣٠) هـ أو (١٣١) هـ انظر ترجمته في سير أعلام النبلاء ٥/٣٥٣-٣٦١.

(٣٥) في المطبوع: «لا نكاد نسأله عن حديث».

When ʿAbd al-Raḥmān ibn al-Qāsim (the great-grandson of Abū Bakr al-Ṣiddīq) mentioned the Prophet ﷺ, it seemed as if the blood had drained from his face because it had become so pale, and his tongue had become dry in his mouth out of awe for the Messenger of Allah ﷺ.

I used to visit Amīr ibn ʿAbdullāh ibn al-Zubayr, and when the Prophet ﷺ was mentioned in his presence, he would weep so much that his eyes had no tears left to cry.

I saw Imam al-Zuhrī, who was one of the most easy-going and friendly people to people, but when the Prophet ﷺ was mentioned in his presence, it was as if he did not know you and you did not know him.

I used to visit Ṣafwān ibn Sulaym who was one of those who performed abundant amounts of worship to Allah. When the Prophet ﷺ was mentioned to him he would weep, and he would not stop weeping until people had to get up and disperse from around him and leave him."

It is related that when Qatādah heard a hadith, he began to cry and sob loudly, becoming very distressed to the extent that he could not stay still in one place.

When large crowds started to gather around Imam Mālik (who famously taught hadith in Masjid Nabawī ﷺ nearby the grave of Rasūlullāh ﷺ) to learn from him, it was said to him: "If only you would appoint someone in your gathering (i.e. sitting very close to you) to whom you could dictate to, and then he could make people hear (by raising his voice and relating what you are teaching) it would be better." He replied: "Allah said: 'O you who believe, do not raise your voices above the voice of the Prophet' (Ḥujurāt 49:2). The

وقد اختلفتُ إليه[٣٦] زَماناً فما كنتُ أراه إلا علىٰ ثلاث خِصَال: إمّا مُصَلِّيًا، وإمّا صامتًا؛ وإمّا يقرأُ القُرآن؛ ولا يتكلّم فيما لا يَعْنيه؛ وكان من العلماء والعُبَّادِ الذين يَخْشَوْنَ اللهَ عزَّ وجَلَّ.

ولقد كان عَبْدُ الرحمن بن القاسم[٣٧] يذكُرُ النبيَّ ﷺ فيُنْظَرُ إلىٰ لونه كأنه نُزِفَ منه الدَّمُ، ولقد جفَّ لسانهُ في فَمِه هَيْبَةً لرسُولِ الله ﷺ.

ولقد كنتُ آتِي عامِرَ بن عَبْد الله بن الزُّبَيْر[٣٨] فإذا ذُكِر عِنْده النبيُّ ﷺ بكىٰ حتى لا يَبْقَى في عينيْهِ دُموع. ولقد رأيتُ الزُّهْرِيَّ، وكان من أَهنأ الناسِ وأقربِهم، فإذا ذُكِر عنده النبيُّ ﷺ فكأنه ما عَرَفك ولا عَرَفْتَهُ.

ولقد كنتُ آتِي صَفْوَان بن سُلَيم[٣٩]، وكان من المتعبّدين المجتهدين؛ فإذا ذُكِر عنده النبيُّ ﷺ بكىٰ، فلا يزالُ يبكي حتى يقومَ الناسُ عنه ويتركوه. ورُوِيَ عَنْ قتادة أنه كان إذا سَمِعَ الحديثَ أَخذه العَوِيلُ والزَّويل. ولما كَثُر علىٰ مالكٍ الناسُ قيل له: لو جَعلْتَ مُسْتَمْلِياً[٤٠] يُسْمِعُهم؟ فقال: قال الله تعالىٰ: ﴿لَا تَرْفَعُوٓاْ أَصْوَٰتَكُمْ فَوْقَ صَوْتِ

---

(٣٦) اختلفتُ إليه: تردَّدْتُ إليه.

(٣٧) هو عبد الرحمن بن القاسم بن محمد بن أبي بكر الصديق، إمام، ثبت، فقيه، عداده في صغار التابعين. ولد في خلافة معاوية، ومات سنة (١٢٦) هـ انظر ترجمته في سير أعلام النبلاء (٦/٥-٦).

(٣٨) إمام ربّاني، ثقة عابد. روىٰ له الستة. توفي سنة (١٢١) هـ انظر ترجمته في سير أعلام النبلاء ٥/٢١٩-٢٢٠.

(٣٩) إمام، ثقة، حافظ، فقيه، عابد. مات سنة (١٣٢) هـ وعاش (٧٢) سنة. انظر ترجمته في سير أعلام النبلاء ٥/٣٦٤-٣٦٨.

(٤٠) مستملياً: أي رجلاً تملي عليه الحديث ثم يقوم بتبليغه.

respect due to the Prophet ﷺ after his passing is the same respect due to him when he was alive."

Ibn Sīrīn ؒ used to laugh at times, but when the hadiths of the Prophet ﷺ were mentioned in his presence he became humble.

When a hadith of the Prophet ﷺ was recited, 'Abd al-Raḥmān ibn Mahdī ؒ commanded them to be silent, saying: "Do not raise your voices above the voice of the Prophet" (Ḥujurāt 49:2). He interpreted the above *āyāh* to mean that people must be completely silent when the Prophet's hadiths are being recited, as if they were listening to the Prophet ﷺ speak directly.

ٱلنَّبِيِّ﴾ [الحجرات: ٢] وحُرْمتُه حيّاً وميتاً سواء.[وكان ابْنُ سِيرين ربما يَضْحَكُ؛ فإذا ذُكِرَ عنده حديثُ النبيِّ ﷺ خَشَع][٤١].

وكان عَبْدُ الرحمن بن مَهْدِي[٤٢] إذا قرأ حديثَ النبيِّ ﷺ أَمرهم بالسكوت؛ وقال: ﴿لَا تَرْفَعُوٓاْ أَصْوَٰتَكُمْ فَوْقَ صَوْتِ ٱلنَّبِيِّ﴾ [الحجرات: ٢] وَيَتَأَوَّل أنه يجبُ له من الإنصات عند قراءة حديثه ما يجبُ له عِنْدَ سَمَاع قوله.

---

(٤١) سيعيده المصنف في الفصل التالي.

(٤٢) هو سيد الحفَّاظ، كان إماماً، ناقداً، مجوِّداً، ثبتاً. ولد سنة (١٣٥) هـ وتوفي سنة (١٩٨) هـ انظر ترجمته في سير أعلام النبلاء ٩/١٩٢-٢٠٩.

Section Four

The Salaf's Respect (*Ta'ẓīm*) for the Transmission of the Prophet's Hadiths and His Sunnah

1269– 'Amr ibn Maymūn said: "I frequently visited 'Abdullāh ibn Mas'ūd over the course of a year, and I never heard him say: 'The Messenger of Allah ﷺ said..." except for one day, he uttered with his tongue: "The Messenger of Allah ﷺ said..." then all of a sudden he was overtaken with great distress until I started seeing beads of sweat falling from his forehead. Then he said: "Like this, *inshā'Āllah*" or he said: "more than this..." or "less than this..." or "close to this..." (Ḥākim 3/214)

Another narration has it: "...until his face became extremely red (i.e. almost dark red from the intensity of his distress and sadness)."

In another narration: "...until tears were flowing down from his eyes, and his jugular veins were bulging [because of the intensity of his love and emotion...]"

Ibrāhīm ibn 'Abdullāh in Quraym al-Anṣārī, the Qāḍī of Medina, said: "Imam Mālik ibn Anas passed by Abū Hāzim while he was teaching hadiths, and Abū Hāzim gave him permission to listen. But Imam Mālik said: 'I cannot find a place to sit, and I strongly dislike listening to the hadith of the Messenger of Allah while standing up.'"

فصل

فِيْ سِيْرَةِ السَّلَفِ فِي تَعْظِيمِ رِوَايَةِ حَدِيْثِ رَسُوْلِ اللهِ ﷺ وسُنَّتِهِ[٤٣]

١٢٦٩- حدثنا الحُسين بن محمد الحافظ، حدثنا أبو الفضل بن خَيْرُون، حدثنا أبو بكر البَرْقَانِي، وغَيْرُه، حدثنا أبو الحسن الدارَقُطني، حدثنا علي بن مُبَشِّر، حدثنا أحمد بن سِنَان القطّان، أخبرنا يزيد بن هارون، أخبرنا المسعودي، عن مُسلم البَطِين، عن عَمْرِو بن مَيْمُون؛ قال: اختلفتُ إلىٰ ابْنِ مسعود سَنَةً؛ فما سمعتهُ يقول: قال رسولُ الله صلى الله عليه وسلم، إلاَّ أَنه حدَّث يوماً فجرىٰ علىٰ لسانه: قال رسولُ الله ﷺ، ثم عَلاَهُ كَرْبٌ، حتى رأَيتُ العَرَقَ يتحدَّر عن جَبهته، ثم قال: هكذا إنْ شاء الله، أو فَوْق ذا، أَو ما دُونَ ذَا، أو ما هو قريبٌ مِنْ ذَا. وفي رواية: فتربَّدَ وَجهه. وفي رواية: وقد تغَرْغرتْ عَيْنَاه، وانتفَخَتْ أَوداجُه. وقال إبراهيم بن عبد الله بن قُرَيْم الأنصاري، قاضي المدينة: مَرّ مالكُ بن أَنَس علىٰ أَبِي حازم، وهو يحدِّثُ، فجازَهُ، وقال: إني لم أَجِدْ مَوْضِعاً أَجلِسُ فيه، وكرهتُ أَنْ آخُذَ حديثَ رسول الله ﷺ وأنا قائم. وقال مالك:

---

(٤٣) في المطبوع: «وسننه».

Imam Mālik ﷺ said: "A man came to Sa'īd ibn al-Musayyab ﷺ and asked him about a hadith while he was reclining, so he sat up and related the hadith to him. The man said to him: 'I wish you hadn't troubled yourself.' He retorted: 'I strongly dislike relating to you hadith from the Messenger of Allah ﷺ while I am reclining.'"

It is related that Imam Muhammad ibn Sīrīn ﷺ used to laugh, but when the hadith of the Prophet ﷺ was mentioned in his presence, he became humble and serious.

Abū Muṣ'ab ﷺ said: "Mālik ibn Anas ﷺ would not relate the hadith of the Messenger of Allah ﷺ except in a state of *wuḍū'* out of respect (*ta'ẓīm*) for the Prophet ﷺ."

Muṣ'ab ibn 'Abdullāh said: "When Imam Mālik ibn Anas would speak about the Messenger of Allah ﷺ, he would first perform *wuḍū'*, get himself ready, put on his clothes, and then relate the hadith. He was asked about why he does all that, and he said, "It is because it is the hadith of the Messenger of Allah ﷺ."

Muṭarrif (the son of Imam Mālik's sister) said: "When people came to visit Imam Mālik, his slave girl would come out to them and ask: 'The sheikh is asking you whether you want to hear hadiths or you have other questions (i.e. *fiqh*).' If they had questions, he would come out to them immediately. But if they came for hadiths, he would first perform ghusl, apply perfume, put on fresh clothes, wear a dark green cloak, a turban, and put the hood of his cloak on his head. A chair would be placed for him, then he would come out and sit on it in a state of complete humility, and wood-*bakhūr* (aloeswood) would be kept continuously burning during the session until he had finished teaching the hadiths of the Messenger of Allah ﷺ."

Another scholar said: "Imam Mālik would not sit on that chair except to teach the hadith of the Messenger of Allah ﷺ."

جاء رجلٌ إلىٰ ابْنِ المُسَيِّب، فسَأله عن حديثٍ وهو مُضْطَجِعٌ، فجلس وحدَّثَه؛ فقال له الرجُلُ: وَدِدْت أَنكَ لم تتَعَنَّ[٤٤]، فقال[٤٥]: إني كرهتُ أَنْ أُحدِّثكَ عن رسولِ اللهِ ﷺ وأنا مُضْطَجع. ورُوي عن محمد بن سيرين أَنه قد يكونُ يضحكُ، فإذا ذُكِرَ عنده حديثُ النبيّ ﷺ خَشَع. وقال أبو مُصْعب: كان مالكُ بن أَنَس لا يُحدِّثُ بحديثِ رسولِ اللهِ ﷺ إلاَّ وهو علىٰ وُضوءٍ، إجلالاً له. وحكىٰ مالكٌ ذلك عن جعفر بن محمد الصادق. وقال مُصْعَب بن عبد الله: كان مالك بن أَنَس إذا حدَّث عن رسولِ اللهِ ﷺ توضَّأ وتَهيَّأ، ولبِسَ ثيابَه، ثم يحدِّث. قال مُصْعب: فسُئل عن ذلك، فقال: إنه حديثُ رسولِ اللهِ ﷺ. قال مُطَرِّفٌ: كان إذا أَتى الناسُ مالكاً خرجَتْ إليهم الجاريةُ وتقول لهم (١٢٢/ب): يقولُ لكم الشيخُ: تُرِيدون الحديثَ أو المسائل؟ فإنْ قالوا: المسائل خرج إليهم، وإنْ قالوا: الحديث، دخل مُغْتَسَله، فاغتسل وتطَيَّبَ، ولبس ثياباً جُدُداً، ولبس ساجَه وتعمَّمَ، ووضَع علىٰ رأسه رداءَه، وتُلْقىٰ له مِنَصَّةٌ، فيخرج فيجلسُ عليها، وعليه الخشوع، ولا يزالُ يُبَخَّرُ بالعودِ حتى يَفرُغَ منْ حديثِ رسولِ اللهِ ﷺ. قال غَيْرُهُ: ولم يكن يجلسُ علىٰ تلك المِنصَّةِ إلا إذا حدَّث عن رسولِ اللهِ ﷺ.

قال ابنُ أبي أُوَيْس[٤٦]: فقيل لمالك في ذلك، فقال: أُحِبُّ أَنْ أُعظّمَ

---

(٤٤) لم تتعنَّ: أي لم تتعب نفسك.

(٤٥) في الأصل: «قال»، والمثبت من المطبوع.

(٤٦) هو إسماعيل بن عبد الله بن أويس الأصبحي المدني. إمام حافظ، صدوق. ولد سنة (١٣٩) هـ ومات

Ibn Abī Uways ﷺ said: "Imam Mālik was asked about doing all that, and he said: 'I like to show respect (*ta'ẓīm*) for the hadiths of the Messenger of Allah ﷺ. I will not teach hadiths except in a state of purity (*ṭahārah*)."

He also said: "Imam Mālik ﷺ strongly disliked teaching hadiths in the street, while he was standing up, or when he was in a hurry."

He also said: "I like to ensure people truly understand the hadith of the Messenger of Allah ﷺ."

Ḍirār ibn Murrah ﷺ said: "They (the Salaf) would strongly dislike relating hadiths without being in *wuḍū'*."

Qatādah also relates a similar report.

If al-A'mash wanted to teach a hadith when he was not in *wuḍū'*, he would perform *tayammum* (dry ablution).

Qatādah would not mention hadith [from memory] except in the state of purity (*ṭahārah*), and he would not read the hadiths of the Prophet ﷺ [from a book] except in the state of *wuḍū'*.

'Abdullāh ibn al-Mubārak ﷺ said: "I was with Imam Mālik while he was teaching us hadith, and a scorpion stung him 16 times. His colour changed and he turned very pale, but he did not interrupt the hadiths of the Messenger of Allah ﷺ. When he finished the session and everyone had departed, I said to him: "O Abū 'Abdullāh! I saw something extraordinary from you today." He said: "Yes, [the scorpion stung me 16 times, and I was bearing that patiently], and the only reason I bore it so patently was out of respect (*ta'ẓīm*) for the Messenger of Allah ﷺ.""

Ibn Mahdī ﷺ said: "One day I walked with Imam Mālik to the Valley of 'Aqiq and I asked him about a hadith and he scolded me, saying:

حديثَ رسولِ الله ﷺ، ولا أُحدِّثُ به إلا علىٰ طهارةٍ مُتَمَكّناً. قال: وكان يكرهُ أَنْ يحدِّثَ في الطريق، أو وهو قائم، أو مُسْتَعْجل. وقال: أُحِبُّ أَنْ أُفَهِّمَ حديثَ رسولِ الله ﷺ. قال ضِرَارُ بن مُرَّة[٤٧]: كانوا يكرهون أَنْ يحدِّثوا [بحديثٍ] علىٰ غير وُضوء. ونَحْوُه عن قَتَادة. وكان الأَعمشُ[٤٨] إذا أحبَّ أن يحدِّث[٤٩] وهو علىٰ غير وُضُوء تيَمَّم.

وكان قَتَادةُ لا يحدّث إلا علىٰ طهارةٍ، ولا يقرأُ حديثَ النبيِّ ﷺ إلا علىٰ وُضُوء. قال عبد الله بن المبارك: كنتُ عند مالك، وهو يحدِّثنا، فلدغَتْه عَقْرَبٌ ستَّ عَشْرةَ مَرَّةً[٥٠]، وهو يتغيَّرُ لونُه وَيَصْفَرُّ ولا يقْطَعُ حديثَ رسولِ الله ﷺ. فلما فرغ من المجلس، وتفرَّقَ عنه الناسُ قلتُ له: يا أَبا عبد الله! لقد رأيتُ منك اليومَ عجَباً؟ قال: نعَمْ [لدغتني عقرب سِتَّ عَشْرَةَ مرَّةً، وأَنا صابرٌ في جميع ذلك؛ [و] إنما صَبَرْتُ إِجلالاً لحديثِ رسولِ الله ﷺ. قال ابْنُ مهدي[٥١]: مشيتُ يوماً مع

سنة (٢٢٦) هـ وقيل (٢٢٧) هـ. انظر ترجمته في سير أعلام النبلاء ١٠/٣٩١-٣٩٥.

(٤٧) ثقة، ثبت، فاضل. حفر قبره قبل موته بـ (١٥) سنة، وكان يأتيه فيختم فيه القرآن. توفي سنة (١٣٢) هـ انظر تهذيب الكمال وفروعه.

(٤٨) هو سليمان بن مِهْران الأعمش، الإمام، شيخ الإسلام، شيخ المقرئين والمحدثين. ولد سنة (٦١) هـ ومات سنة (١٤٧) أو (١٤٨) هـ. انظر ترجمته في سير أعلام النبلاء ٦/٢٢٦-٢٤٩.

(٤٩) في المطبوع: «إذا حدَّث وهو... ».

(٥٠) في الأصل: «ستة عشر مرةً»، والمثبت من المطبوع، وهو الصواب.

(٥١) تحرَّف في الأصل إلىٰ: «ابن مُهَذَّبٍ»، والمثبت من المطبوع.

'You are too good in my eyes to ask about a hadith of the Messenger of Allah ﷺ while we are walking!'"

On one occasion, Qāḍī Jarīr ibn 'Abd al-Hamid asked Imam Mālik ﷺ about a hadith while he was standing up, and Imam Mālik ordered that he should be arrested for that. He was told, "But he is a Qāḍī!" He retorted, "A Qāḍī should have more *adab* (manners)!"

Hishām ibn al-Ghāzī/Hishām ibn 'Ammār al-Qāri' asked Imam Mālik about a hadith while standing up, and Imam Mālik struck him 20 times with a whip. Then he had pity on him and taught him 20 hadiths. Hishām said: "I wish that he had given me more hits, and then taught me more hadiths!"

'Abdullāh ibn Ṣāliḥ ﷺ said: "Mālik and al-Layth ﷺ only wrote down hadiths when they were in a state of purity (*ṭahārah*)."

Qatādah used to recommend to not read the hadiths of the Prophet ﷺ [from a book] except in the state of *wuḍū'*, and he would not verbally relate hadith except in a state of purity (*ṭahārah*).

مالك إلىٰ العَقِيق، فسألتُه عن حديثٍ، فانتهرني[٥٢] وقال [لي]: كنتَ في عيني أجلَّ [من] أَنْ تسألَني عن حديثِ رسولِ الله ﷺ ونحنُ نمشي. وسأَله جرير بن عبد الحميد القاضي عن حديثٍ وهو قائم، فأَمر بحَبْسه، فقيل، له: إنه قاضٍ! قال: القاضي أَحقُّ مَنْ أُدِّب. وذُكِر أَن هشام بن الغازي[٥٣] سأَل مالكاً عن حديثٍ وهو واقفٌ فضربه عشرين سَوْطاً، ثم أَشفق [عليه] فحدَّثه عشرين حديثاً؛ فقال هشام: وددْتُ لو زادني سِيَاطاً ويزيدني حديثاً. قال عَبْدُ الله بن صالح[٥٤]: كان مالكٌ واللَّيثُ[٥٥] لا يكتبان الحديثَ إلاَّ وهما طاهِرَان. وكان قتادةُ يستحبُّ [١٢٣/أ] ألاَّ يَقْرأَ أَحاديث النبيّ ﷺ إلا علىٰ وضوءٍ، ولا يحدِّثُ به إلاَّ علىٰ طَهَارةٍ. وكان الأعمشُ إذا أَراد أَنْ يحدِّثَ وهو علىٰ غير وضوءٍ تيمَّم.

---

(٥٢) (انتهرني): زجرني.

(٥٣) إمام مقرئ محدث. مات سنة (١٥٦) أو (١٥٣) هـ مترجم في سير أعلام النبلاء ٦٠/٧. ولا يعلم له رواية عن الإمام مالك. ولعلَّ الصواب: «هشام بن عمار القارىء» فقد قال الذهبي في سير أعلام النبلاء (٤٢٠/١١): «سمع من مالكٍ، وتمَّتْ له معه قصة».

(٥٤) هو كاتب الليث بن سعد، إمام، محدث، من أوعية العلم. ولد سنة (١٣٧) هـ ومات سنة (٢٢٣) هـ انظر ترجمته في السير ٤٠٥/١٠-٤١٦.

(٥٥) (اللَّيث): هو ابن سعد. إمام، مجتهد مطلق. مات سنة (١٧٥ هـ انظر ترجمته في سير أعلام النبلاء ١٣٦/٨-١٦٣.

SECTION FIVE

Part of Respecting the Prophet ﷺ is Respecting His Family, His Descendants, and His Wives, as He Enjoined and as Demonstrated by the Salaf al-Ṣāliḥ

Allah said: "Allah wants to remove impurity from you, O People of the House." (Aḥzāb 33:33).

He said: "His wives are their mothers." (Aḥzāb 33:6).

AHL AL-BAYT

1270 – Zayd ibn Arqam related that the Messenger of Allah ﷺ said: "I implore you by Allah! The People of my House! The People of my House! The People of my House! (*Ahl Baytī! Ahl Baytī! Ahl Baytī!*)." We asked Zayd: "Who are the People of the Prophet's House?" and he said: "The family of 'Alī ibn Abī Ṭālib, the family of Ja'far, the family of 'Aqīl, and the family of al-'Abbās." (Muslim 2408)

1271 – The Prophet ﷺ said: "I am leaving you something; as long as you hold fast to it, you will not go astray: The Book of Allah, and my family (*'itratī*) – the People of my House (Ahl Baytī). So, be careful how you treat those two things after me." (Tirmidhī 3788)

1272 – The Prophet ﷺ said: "Recognition of the family of Muhammad is freedom from the Fire. Love of the family of Muhammad is crossing over the Ṣirāṭ. Helping the family of Muhammad is safety from the Fire." (Suyūṭī's al-Manāhil)

فصل

ومن تَوْقيره ﷺ وبِرّه - بِرُّ آلِه وذُرِّيَّته وأُمَّهاتِ المؤمنين: أزواجِه، كما حضَّ عليه ﷺ، وسلكهُ السلفُ الصالحُ رضِيَ اللهُ عنهم

قال اللهُ تعالىٰ: ﴿إِنَّمَا يُرِيدُ ٱللَّهُ لِيُذۡهِبَ عَنكُمُ ٱلرِّجۡسَ أَهۡلَ ٱلۡبَيۡتِ وَيُطَهِّرَكُمۡ تَطۡهِيرٗا﴾ [الأحزاب: ٣٣]. و قال تعالىٰ: ﴿وَأَزۡوَٰجُهُۥٓ أُمَّهَٰتُهُمۡۗ﴾ [الأحزاب: ٦].

١٢٧٠- أَخبرنا الشيخ أبو محمدِ بن أحمد العَدْل مِنْ[٥٦] كتابِه، وكتَبْتُ من أصله، حدثنا أبو الحسن المقرئ الفَرْغاني، حدثتني أُمُّ القاسم بنت الشيخ أبي[٥٧] بكر الخفَّاف، قالت: حدثني أبي، حدثنا حاتم - وهو ابن عقيل، حدثنا يحيىٰ: هو ابن إسماعيل، حدثنا يحيىٰ: هو الحِمّاني، حدثنا وَكيع، عن أبيه، عن سَعِيد بن مسروق، عن يزيد بن حَيّان، عن زَيد بن أَرْقَمَ؛ قال: قال رسولُ اللهِ ﷺ: «**أَنْشُدُكُمُ اللهَ في[٥٨] أَهل**

(٥٦) في الأصل: «في». والمثبت من المطبوع.

(٥٧) في الأصل: «أبو»، والمثبت من المطبوع، وهو الصواب.

(٥٨) كلمة: «في»، لم ترد في المطبوع.

One of the ulema said: "'Recognition' in this case means recognizing the close relationship and high rank of Ahl al-Bayt in relation to the Prophet ﷺ. And if one recognizes them because of that, then one will also recognize the rights and respect that are owed to them because of the Prophet ﷺ."

1273 – 'Umar ibn Abī Salamah said that when Allah revealed the verse: "Allah wants to remove impurity from you, O People of the House" (Aḥzāb 33:33) – and it was revealed in Umm Salamah's house – the Prophet a summoned Fāṭimah, Ḥasan and Ḥusayn, and covered them in a shawl (*kisa'*) and 'Alī was behind him (and he ﷺ also covered 'Alī too).[4] Then he ﷺ said: "O Allah! These are the People of my House (Ahl Baytī), so remove all impurity from them and purify them completely." (Tirmidhī 3787)

1274 – Sa'd ibn Abī Waqqāṣ ﷺ said that when the *āyāh* of mutual cursing[5] (*mubāhalah*) was revealed, the Prophet ﷺ called 'Alī, Hassan, Ḥusayn and Fāṭimah, and said: "O Allah, these are my family (Ahl Baytī)." (Muslim 32/2404)

'ALĪ IBN ABĪ ṬĀLIB ﷺ

1275 – The Prophet ﷺ said about 'Alī ﷺ: "Whoever takes me for a master, then 'Alī is also his master. O Allah, befriend the one who befriends him and oppose the one who opposes him!"

---

4 Translator's Note: This is an addition from *Sunan al-Tirmidhī* that is not in *Jāmi' al-Usūl*, and perhaps that addition is from the different manuscripts.

5 The *āyah* of *mubāhalah* (mutual cursing) is: "And whosoever disputes with you concerning him after the knowledge that has come to you, say, 'Come, let us call our sons and your sons, our wives and your wives, ourselves and your selves, then let us humbly pray and so lay the curse of Allah upon the ones who lie.'"(Āl-'Imrān 3:61)

بيتي...» ثلاثاً. قلنا لزَيْد: مَنْ أَهْلُ بيتِه؟ قال: آلُ عليٍّ بن أبي طالب، وآلُ جَعْفَرٍ، وآل عَقِيلٍ، وآلُ العباس(٥٩).

١٢٧١- وقال عليه السلام: «إني تَارِكٌ فيكم ما إنْ أخذتُم به لم تضِلُّوا: كتابَ الله، وعِتْرتي: أهلَ بيتي ؛ فانْظُرُوا كيف تَخْلُفوني فيهما» (٦٠).

١٢٧٢- وقال عليه السلام: «معرفةُ آلِ محمدٍ [صلى الله عليه وسلم] براءةٌ من النار، وحُبُّ آلِ محمد - صلى الله عليه وسلم - جوازٌ على الصِّراطِ، والوَلايةُ لآل محمدٍ أمانٌ من العذاب» (٦١). قال بعضُ العلماء: معرفتُهم هي معرفةُ مكانِهم من النبيّ صلى الله عليه وسلم، وإذا عَرَفَهُمْ بذلك عرفَ وُجوبَ [حقّهم و] حُرمَتهم بسببه.

١٢٧٣- وعن عُمَرَ بن أبي سَلَمةَ: لما نزلت: ﴿إِنَّمَا يُرِيدُ ٱللَّهُ لِيُذۡهِبَ عَنكُمُ ٱلرِّجۡسَ أَهۡلَ ٱلۡبَيۡتِ وَيُطَهِّرَكُمۡ تَطۡهِيرٗا﴾ [الأحزاب: ٣٣] - وذلك في بيت أمِّ سلمَة - دعا فاطمة وحَسَنا وحُسينا، فجلَّلهم بكساءٍ، وعليٌّ خَلْفَ ظهره [فجلَّله بكساءٍ](٦٢)، ثم قال: **«اللَّهُمَّ! هؤلاء أهلُ بيتي ؛ فأَذْهِبْ عنهم الرِّجْسَ، وطَهِّرْهُم تطهيراً»** (٦٣).

---

(٥٩) أخرجه مسلم (٢٤٠٨).

(٦٠) أخرجه الترمذي (٣٧٨٨) من حديث زيد بن أرقم وأبي سعيد الخدري. وقال الترمذي: «هذا حديث حسن غريب». وقال السمهودي - كما في فيض القدير ١٥/٣ -: «وفي الباب مايزيد على عشرين من الصحابة». وانظر صحيح مسلم (٢٤٠٨). (عترتي): تقدم شرحها.

(٦١) أورده السيوطي في المناهل (١٠٠٣)، ولم يذكر من خرَّجه. (الوَلاَية): النُّصْرَةُ.

(٦٢) زيادة من سنن الترمذي. وهي ليست موجودة في جامع الأصول ١٥٦/٩. ولعل ذلك من اختلاف النسخ.

(٦٣) أخرجه الترمذي (٣٧٨٧) وقال: «وهذا حديث غريب من هذا الوجه» وقال أيضاً: وفي الباب عن أم سلمة، ومعقل بن يسار، وأبي الحمراء، وأنس. (الرجس): النجس، وكل ما يستقذر، وقيل هو الإثم/ جامع

1276 – The Prophet ﷺ also said to ʿAlī ﷺ: "None will love you except a believer (*mu'min*), and none will hate you except a hypocrite (*munāfiq*)." (Muslim 78)

ʿABBĀS IBN ʿABD AL-MUṬṬALIB ﷺ

1277 – The Prophet ﷺ said to al-'Abbās ﷺ: "I swear by the One Who controls my soul, belief (*īmān)* will not enter a man's heart until he loves you for the sake of Allah and His Messenger. And whoever harms my uncle has harmed me; a man's uncle is like his father." (Tirmidhī 3758)

1278 – The Prophet ﷺ also said to al-'Abbās ﷺ: "Feed ʿAlī along with your children, O my dear uncle." Then he gathered them and wrapped them with his shawl, saying, "This is my uncle, a copy of my father, and these are the people of my house, so veil them from the Fire as I am veiling them." Then the lintel[6] of the door and the walls of the house said: "*Āmīn! Āmīn!*" (Bukhārī 3735)

ḤASAN, ḤUSAYN, AND USĀMAH

1279 – The Prophet ﷺ used to take the hand of Usāmah ibn Zayd ﷺ and al-Ḥasan e and say: "O Allah, I love truly love them, so You love them." (Bukhārī 3735)

1280 – Abū Bakr al-Ṣiddīq ﷺ said: "Take care of Muhammad by respecting the People of his House (*Ahl Baytīhī*)."[7]

---

6 Translator's Note: Lintel refers to a horizontal support of timber, stone, concrete, or steel across the top of a door or window.

7 Bukhārī 3713. Hafiz Ibn Ḥajar al-'Asqalānī states in Fatḥ al-Bārī (7/79): "Abū Bakr ﷺ is addressing all people by that and he is strongly counselling them with this advice. Doing *'murāqabah'* of something refers to preserving it. His statement means: Protect Ahl al-Bayt, and do not hurt them or do any evil to them."

١٢٧٤- وعن سعد بن أبي وقَّاص (١٢٣/ب): لما نزلت آيةُ المُبَاهَلة دعا النبيُّ ﷺ عَلِيّا وحَسَناً وحُسيناً وفاطمة، وقال: «**اللَّهُمَّ! هؤلاء أهلي**»[٦٤].

١٢٧٥- وقال النبيُّ ﷺ في عليّ: «**مَنْ كنتُ مَوْلاه فعليٌّ مولاه ؛ اللهم! وَالِ مَنْ وَالاَهُ، وَعَادِ مَنْ عَادَاهُ**»[٦٥].

١٢٧٦- وقال فيه: «**لا يحبُّكَ إلاّ مُؤمنٌ، ولا يُبْغضُك إلا مُنافقٌ**»[٦٦]

١٢٧٧- وقال للعبّاس: «**والذي نفسي بيده! لا يَدْخُلُ قَلْبَ رجُلٍ الإِيمانُ حتى يُحبَّكم للهِ ورسُولِه. ومَنْ آذىٰ عَمّي فقد آذَاني ؛ وإنما عَمُّ الرجلِ صِنْوُ أبيه**»[٦٧].

١٢٧٨- وقال للعباس: «**اغْدُ عليَّ يا عمّ! مع وَلدك**» فجمعهم وجَلَّلَهم بمُلاَءَتِهِ، ثم قال: «**هذا عَمّي وصِنْوُ أبي ؛ وهؤلاءِ أهلُ بيتي ؛ فاسْتُرْهم اللَّهُمَّ! من النار كسَتْرِي إياهم**» فأَمَّنَتْ أُسْكُفَّةُ الباب

الأصول ١٥٥/٩.

(٦٤) أخرجه مسلم (٣٢/٢٤٠٤).

(٦٥) تقدم برقم (٦٤٤).

(٦٦) أخرجه مسلم (٧٨) عن علي قال: «إنه لعهد النبي الأمي - ﷺ - إليَّ أن لا يحبني إلا مؤمن ولا يبغضني إلا منافق».

(٦٧) أخرجه الترمذي (٣٧٥٨) من حديث عبد المطلب بن ربيعة. وقال الترمذي: «هذا حديث حسن صحيح». (الصِّنوُ): المِثْلُ/ جامع الأصول ٢٢/٩.

1281 – Abū Bakr al-Ṣiddīq also said: "I swear by the One Who controls my soul, keeping a connection alive between myself and the relatives of the Messenger of Allah ﷺ is more beloved to me than keeping the connection with my own kinsfolk." (Bukhārī 3712; Muslim 1759)

1282 – The Prophet ﷺ said: "Allah loves those who love Ḥusayn."

1283 – The Prophet ﷺ also said: "Whoever loves me and loves these two (and he indicated towards Ḥasan and Ḥusayn and their father and mother) will be with me on my level on the Day of Judgement."

QURAISH

1284 – The Prophet ﷺ said: "Whoever disrespects Quraysh, Allah will abase him." (Aḥmad 1/64)

1285 – The Prophet ﷺ said: "Give preference to Quraysh and do not precede them." (Bazzar 2784)

1286 – The Prophet ﷺ said to Umm Salamah : "Do not hurt my me regarding 'Ā'ishah." (Bukhārī 2571)

1287 – 'Uqbah ibn al-Ḥārith said: "I saw Abū Bakr putting al-Ḥasan ibn 'Alī on his shoulders, saying lightheartedly: "By my father, he resembles the Prophet! He does not resemble 'Alī!" and 'Alī was laughing. (Bukhārī 3750)

1288 – It is related that 'Abdullāh ibn Ḥasan (the great-grandson of 'Alī Ibn Abī Ṭālib) said: "I came to 'Umar ibn 'Abd al-'Azīz for something I needed, and he said: "If you have a need, then send for

وحوائطُ البيت: آمين. آمين[٦٨].

١٢٧٩- وكان يأخذ أُسامةَ بن زَيْد، والْحَسَن؛ ويقول: «**اللَّهُمَّ! إني أُحبُّهما فَأَحِبَّهُما**»[٦٩].

١٢٨٠- وقال أبو بكر: ارْقُبُوا محمَّداً في أهل بيته[٧٠].

١٢٨١- وقال أيضاً: والذي نَفْسِي بيده! لَقَرابةُ رسولِ الله ﷺ أحبُّ إليّ أنْ أصِلَ مِن قرابتي.

١٢٨٢- وقال[٧١] ﷺ: «**أَحَبَّ اللهُ مَنْ أحبَّ حُسيناً**»[٧٢].

١٢٨٣- وقال: «**من أحبّني وأَحَبَّ هذين** - وأشار إلىٰ حَسَنٍ وحُسَين وأباهما وأُمَّهما - **كان معي في دَرجتي يوم القيامة**»[٧٣].

١٢٨٤- وقال عليه السلام: «**مَنْ أهان قُريشاً أهانه اللهُ**».

١٢٨٥- وقال [ﷺ]: «**قَدِّموا قُريشاً ولا تَقَدَّموها**».

---

(٦٨) تقدم برقم (٧٨١). (جَلَّلهم): غطَّاهم. (ملاءة): ملحفة. (أُسْكُفَّة البابِ): عَتَبَتُهُ.

(٦٩) أخرجه البخاري (٣٧٣٥) من حديث أسامة بن زيد.

(٧٠) أخرجه البخاري (٣٧١٣). قال الحافظ في الفتح ٧٩/٧: «يخاطب بذلك الناس، ويوصيهم به، والمراقبة للشيء: المحافظة عليه، يقول: احفظوه فيهم، فلا تؤذوهم، ولا تسيئوا إليهم».

(٧١) أخرجه الترمذي (٣٧٧٥)، وابن ماجه (١٤٤) من حديث يعلىٰ بن مرة. وقال الترمذي: «هذا حديث حسن». وقد استوفينا تخريجه في موارد الظمآن (٢٢٤٠).

(٧٢) في الأصل: «أحب الله من أحب حسناً، وحسيناً، وأمهما وأباهما»، والمثبت من مصادر التخريج. في المطبوع: «أحب الله من أَحبَّ حَسناً وحُسَيناً».

(٧٣) تقدم برقم (١٢٠٤).

me or write to me, because I am ashamed before Allah to see you at my door."[8]

1289 – Al-Sha'bī ﵀ said: "Zayd ibn Thābit ﷺ led his mother's funeral prayer, and then his mule was brought near so he could mount it. Then Ibn 'Abbās ﷺ came and took hold of the stirrup, and Zayd said: 'Let go of it, O son of the uncle of the Messenger of Allah!' He said: 'This is the way we treat the scholars?' Then Zayd kissed the hand of Ibn 'Abbās apologetically and said: 'This is the way we were commanded to treat the Ahl al-Bayt of our Prophet ﷺ.'" (Ṭabarānī's Kabīr 4746)

1290 – Ibn 'Umar ﷺ saw Muhammad ibn Usāmah ibn Zayd f and, not knowing who he was, said: "If only he were my slave!" He was told: "That is Muhammad ibn Usāmah." Ibn 'Umar ﷺ bowed his head in humility and struck the earth with his hand and said: "If only the Messenger of Allah ﷺ had seen him, he would have loved him." (Bukhārī 3734)

1291 – Imam al-Awzā'ī ﵀ said: "The daughter of Usāmah ibn Zayd ﷺ – the Companion of the Prophet ﷺ – went to see 'Umar ibn 'Abd al-'Azīz and she had an assistant (*mawlā*) of hers with her holding her hand. 'Umar ibn 'Abd al-'Azīz stood up for her and walked to her, then placed his garment over his hands (so as to not to touch her directly which would be impermissible) then put her hand in

---

8 Translator's Note: Because even though 'Umar Ibn 'Abd al-'Azīz ﵀ was the current Caliph and the correct person to ask from, he was ashamed before Allah to have someone from Ahl al-Bayt ﷺ (the Prophet's family) asking for something in public. Similarly, for us, in our times, if we have a hunch that someone from Ahl al-Bayt is in any type of need that we are able to fulfil, then we should hasten to offer that to them out of love for their grandfather, Rasūlullāh ﷺ, and not wait for them to be forced to ask for it. As one scholar stated: "The only reason Allah let us know about the need of the needy is to give us the chance to help them" and we will be asked about that on *Qiyāmah*.

١٢٨٦- وقال عليه السلام لأم سَلَمَةَ: «**لا تؤذيني**[٧٤] **في عائِشَةَ**».

١٢٨٧- وعن عُقْبَة بن الحارث: رأيتُ أبا بكر [رضي الله عنه] وقد جعل الحَسَن بن علي علىٰ عُنقِه وهو يقول: بأَبي شَبِيهٌ بالنبي، ليس شبيهاً بعليّ، وعليٌّ [رضِيَ الله عنه] يَضْحَك.

١٢٨٨-ورُوِي عن عَبْدالله بن الحسَن، قال: أَتَيتُ عُمر بن عبدالعزيز-رضي الله عنه - في حاجة، فقال لي: إذا كانت لك حاجةٌ فأَرسِلْ إليّ أو اكتُبْ؛ فإني أَستحيي من الله أن يراك علىٰ بابي.

١٢٨٩- وعن الشَّعْبِيّ: صلّىٰ زَيْد بن ثابت علىٰ جَنازة أُمه، ثم قُرِّبَت له بَغْلتُه ليركَبَها (١٢٤/أ)، فجاء ابْنُ عباس فأخذ بِرِكَابِه؛ فقال زَيْدٌ: خَلِّ عنه، يا بْنَ عمِّ رسولِ الله! فقال: هكذا نَفْعَلُ بالعلماء. فقَبَّل زَيْد يَدَ ابْن عباس؛ وقال: هكذا أُمرنا أَنْ نَفْعَلَ بأَهل بيتِ نبيّنا.

١٢٩٠- ورأىٰ ابْنُ عُمَرَ محمدَ بن أُسامةَ بن زَيْد؛ فقال: لَيْتَ هذا عَبْدي؛ فقيل له: هو محمد بن أُسامة. فَطأْطَأَ ابنُ عُمَرَ رَأْسَه ونقَر بيده الأَرْض، وقال: لو رآهُ رسولُ اللهِ صلى الله عليه وسلم لأَحَبَّه.

١٢٩١-وقال الأَوْزاعي: دخلَتْ بِنْتُ أُسامةَ بن زَيْدٍ-صاحبِ رسولِ الله صلى الله عليه وسلم - علىٰ عُمر بن عبد العزيز ومعها مَوْلًى لها يُمْسِكُ بيدها، فقام لها عُمر، ومشَىٰ إليها حتى جعل يدَها بين يَدَيْه، ويَدَاه في ثِيَابه. ومَشَىٰ بها

(٧٤) في الأصل: «لا تؤذوني»، والمثبت من المطبوع والبخاري (٢٥٨١).

between his hands. Then he walked with her, sat her in his own place and then sat down in front of her. He did not leave any request she had except that he fulfilled it."

1292 – When 'Umar ibn al-Khaṭṭāb allotted his son 'Abdullāh 3,000 dinars and Usāmah ibn Zayd 3,500 dinars, 'Abdullāh said to his father: "Why did you give him more than me? By Allah, he did not get to the battle ahead of me!" He said: "Because Zayd was dearer to the Messenger of Allah ﷺ than your father, and Usāmah was dearer to him than you, so I prefer to give preference to the love of the Messenger of Allah ﷺ over what I love." (Tirmidhī 3813)

1293 – Mu'āwiyah heard that Kābis ibn Rabī'ah resembled the Messenger of Allah ﷺ, so when he entered unto him in the room, he got up from his seat, met him, and kissed him between the eyes. He gave him *al-Mirghāb* (a valuable piece of land in Basra) as a gift due to his resemblance to the Messenger of Allah ﷺ. (Ibn 'Asākir's Manāhil 1021)

It is related that when Imam Mālik was whipped and beaten by Ja'far ibn Sulaymān (the Abbasid governor of Medina for the Caliph, Ja'far al-Mansur; he was a descendant of al-'Abbās) and he got from him what he got, he was carried away [after being beaten] unconscious. Later when people came to visit him and he regained consciousness, Imam Mālik said: "I testify to you that I have declared the one beating me to be cleared from any crime whatsoever!" Afterwards, he was asked about that and said: "I am afraid of dying and meeting the Prophet ﷺ with the shame that one of his family members will have entered the Fire because of me."

1295 – It is said that the Caliph Mansur said that he could take revenge against Ja'far ibn Sulaymān for whipping Imam Mālik, to which Imam Mālik said to him: "I seek refuge in Allah! I swear by

حتى أَجْلسها علىٰ مَجْلسه، وجلس بين يديها، وماترك لها من حاجَةٍ إلاَّ قَضَاها.

١٢٩٢- ولما فَرض عُمَرُ بن الخطّاب لابْنِه عبدِ اللهِ في ثلاثةِ آلافٍ، ولأُسامة بن زيد في ثلاثة آلاف وخمس مئة، قال عبدُ الله لأبيه: لِمَ فَضَّلْتَه؟ فوالله! ما سبقني إلىٰ مَشْهَد. فقال له: لأَنَّ زيداً كان أَحَبَّ إلىٰ رسولِ الله ﷺ مِنْ أَبيك، وأُسَامةُ أَحبُّ إليه منكَ؛ فآثرتُ حُبَّ رسولِ الله ﷺ علىٰ حُبّي(٧٥).

١٢٩٣- وبلغ معاويةَ: أَنَّ كابِس بن رَبيعة يُشَبَّه برسولِ الله ﷺ؛ فلما دخل عليه من باب الدار قام عن سريره، وتلقَّاه، وقبَّل بين عَيْنيه، وأَقطعه المِرْغابَ لِشَبهه بصورةِ رسولِ الله ﷺ(٧٦).

١٢٩٤- ورُوِي أَن مالكاً - رحِمَه الله - لمّا ضَربه جعفَرُ بن سليمان(٧٧)، ونال منه ما نال، وحُمِل مَغْشيّاً عليه، دخل عليه الناسُ، فأَفَاقَ، فقال: أُشْهِدُكم أَنِّي قد جعلتُ ضاربي في حِلّ. فسُئل بعد ذلك، فقال: خِفْتُ أَن أموتَ، فأَلْقىٰ النبيَّ ﷺ، فأَستَحِي منه أَنْ يدخُلَ بَعْضُ آلِه بِسَبَبِي النار.

---

(٧٥) أخرجه الترمذي (٣٨١٣) وقال: «هذا حديث حسن غريب».

(٧٦) رواه ابن عساكر / المناهل (١٠٢١). المرغاب: موضع بالبصرة/ انظر معجم البلدان ١٠٧/٥-١٠٨.

(٧٧) جعفر بن سليمان بن علي بن عبد الله، ابن عم المنصور، ولي المدينة سنة (١٤٦) هـ ثم مكة معها، ثم عزل فولي البصرة للرشيد. توفي سنة (١٧٤) هـ وقيل سنة (١٧٥) هـ انظر ترجمته في سير أعلام النبلاء ٢٣٩/٨-٢٤٠.

Allah, every time the whip hit my body, I made it halal (lawful) for him to whip me because of his kinship bond with the Messenger of Allah ﷺ."

1296 – Abū Bakr ibn 'Ayyash said: "If Abū Bakr, 'Umar and 'Alī had come to me for something, I would have taken care of 'Alī first due to his kinship to the Messenger of Allah ﷺ. I would rather fall from the heaven to the earth than prefer them over him."

1297 – Someone said to Ibn 'Abbās: "So-and-so has died", referring to one of the Prophet's wives, and Ibn 'Abbās performed *sajdah* (prostration). So people asked him: "Why are you prostrating at this time?" He replied: "Did the Messenger of Allah ﷺ not say: 'When you see a sign, then you all should prostrate?', and what sign could be greater than the passing of one of the wives of the Prophet?" (Abū Dāwūd 1197)

1298 – Abū Bakr and 'Umar used to visit Umm Ayman Barakah, the Prophet's helper, and they would say [about the reason for visiting her]: "The Messenger of Allah ﷺ used to visit her." (Muslim 2454)

1299 – When Ḥalīmah as-Sa'diyyah e – the Prophet's wet-nurse when he was a toddler – came to the Prophet ﷺ when he was an adult, he spread out his cloak for her [to sit on out of respect] and took care of her needs. When the Prophet ﷺ passed away, she came up to Abū Bakr and 'Umar and they did the same for her.

١٢٩٥- وقيل: إنَّ المنصور أقاده من جعفر[٧٨]، فقال له: أَعوذُ باللهِ! (١٢٤/ب) واللهِ! ما ارتفعَ منها سوطٌ عن جسمي إلا وقد جعلتُه في حِلٍّ لقَرَابته من رسول الله ﷺ.

١٢٩٦- وقال أبو بكر بن عَيَّاشٍ[٧٩]: لو أَتاني علي وعمر وأبو بكر[٨٠] لبدأْتُ بحاجةِ عليّ قَبْلهما؛ لقرابته مِنْ رسُولِ الله ﷺ؛ وَلأَنْ أَخِرَّ من السماء إلىٰ الأرض أحبُّ إليَّ مِنْ أَنْ أُقَدِّمَه عليهما.

١٢٩٧- وقيل لابْن عباس: ماتت فلانة - لبعض أزواج النبي ﷺ - فسجد؛ فقيل له: أَتَسجدُ هذه الساعة؟ فقال: أَليس قال رسولُ الله ﷺ: «**إذا رأيتُم آيةً فاسْجُدوا**» وأيُّ آيةٍ أعظمُ من ذهابِ أَزواج النبيّ ﷺ؟

١٢٩٨- وكان أبو بكر وعُمر يَزُورَانِ أُمَّ أَيْمَنَ مولاةَ النبيِّ ﷺ ويقولان: كان رسولُ الله ﷺ يَزُورُها.

١٢٩٩- ولمّا وردَتْ حليمةُ السعديّةُ علىٰ النبيّ ﷺ بسط لها رداءهُ وقَضَىٰ حاجتَها. فلما تُوفِّيَ وفدت علىٰ أَبي بكر وعُمر فصنعا بها مِثْلَ ذلك.

---

(٧٨) (أقاده من جعفر): أي أمر أن يقتص لمالك من جعفر فيضرب كما ضربه.

(٧٩) مختلف في اسمه علىٰ عشرة أقوال. قال ابن حجر: «ثقة عابد، إلا أنه لما كبر ساء حفظه، وكتابه صحيح» مات سنة (١٩٤) هـ أو نحوها وقد قارب المئة. انظر التهذيب وفروعه.

(٨٠) في المطبوع: «أبو بكر وعمر وعلي».

Section Six

Respect for His Companions, Devotion to them and Recognizing what is Due to Them

Part of respecting and obeying the Prophet ﷺ entails respecting his Companions ﷺ, obeying them, recognizing their rights, emulating them, praising them well, asking forgiveness for them, refraining from discussing their differences, and showing enmity to those who are hostile towards them. [It also entails] shunning the false reports of [1] any 'historians', [2] ignorant transmitters, [3] the misguidance of the Shia, or [4] the innovators (*mubtadi'īn*) who detract from any of them. If there is something equivocal, unclear, or ambiguous reported about them regarding the tribulations that took place between them, then one must adopt the best interpretation and look for the most appropriate and befitting way out of it, since that is what they deserve. None of them should be mentioned in a bad manner, nor are they to be rebuked for anything. Rather, we mention their good deeds, their virtues, and their praiseworthy lives, and are silent about all else.

1300 – The Prophet ﷺ said: "When my Companions are mentioned [negatively], refrain." (Haythamī's Majma' al-Zawā'id 7/202)

Allah says: "Muḥammad is the Messenger of Allah. And those with him are firm with the disbelievers and compassionate with one an-

فصل

توقيرُ أَصْحَابِه وَبِرُّهم ومعرفةُ حقِّهم

ومن توقيره وبِرّه [ﷺ] توقيرُ أَصْحَابِه وَبِرُّهم ومعرفةُ حقِّهم، والاقتداءُ بهم، وحُسْنُ الثناء عليهم، والاستغفارُ لهم، والإمساكُ عمَّا شَجَر بينهم، ومعاداةُ مَنْ عادَاهُمْ، والإضرابُ عن أَخبار المؤرِّخين، وجهَلةِ الرُّواةِ، وضُلاَّلِ الشِّيعَة والمُبْتَدِعِين القادحةِ في أحدٍ منهم؛ وأن يُلْتَمس لهم - فيما نُقِل [عنهم] من [مِثْل] ذلك فيما كان بينهم مِنَ الفِتَن - أحسنُ التأويلات، ويُخرَّج لهم أَصْوَبُ المخارج. إِذ هم أهلُ ذلك، ولا يُذكَرُ أحدٌ منهم بسوءٍ، ولا يُغْمَصُ عليه أَمْرُهُ، بل يُذْكَر حسناتُهم وفضائلُهم، وحَمِيدُ سِيرتِهم، ويُسكتُ عما وَرَاءَ ذلك.

١٣٠٠- كما قال عليه السلام: «**إذا ذُكِرَ أَصْحَابِي فأَمسِكُوا**». قال الله تعالى: ﴿مُّحَمَّدٌ رَّسُولُ ٱللَّهِۚ وَٱلَّذِينَ مَعَهُۥٓ أَشِدَّآءُ عَلَى ٱلۡكُفَّارِ رُحَمَآءُ بَيۡنَهُمۡۖ تَرَىٰهُمۡ رُكَّعٗا سُجَّدٗا يَبۡتَغُونَ فَضۡلٗا مِّنَ ٱللَّهِ وَرِضۡوَٰنٗاۖ سِيمَاهُمۡ فِي وُجُوهِهِم مِّنۡ أَثَرِ ٱلسُّجُودِۚ ذَٰلِكَ مَثَلُهُمۡ فِي ٱلتَّوۡرَىٰةِۚ وَمَثَلُهُمۡ فِي ٱلۡإِنجِيلِ كَزَرۡعٍ أَخۡرَجَ شَطۡـَٔهُۥ فَـَٔازَرَهُۥ فَٱسۡتَغۡلَظَ فَٱسۡتَوَىٰ عَلَىٰ

other. You see them bowing and prostrating in prayer, seeking Allah's bounty and pleasure. The sign of brightness can be seen on their faces from the trace of prostrating in prayer. This is their description in the Torah. And their parable in the Gospel is that of a seed that sprouts its tiny branches, making it strong. Then it becomes thick, standing firmly on its stem, to the delight of the planters – in this way Allah makes the believers a source of dismay for the disbelievers. To those of them who believe and do good, Allah has promised forgiveness and a great reward. " (Fatḥ 48:29)

And Allah said: "As for the foremost – the first of the Emigrants and the Helpers and those who follow them in goodness – Allah is pleased with them and they are pleased with Him. And He has prepared for them Gardens under which rivers flow, to stay there for ever and ever. That is the ultimate triumph." (Tawbah 9:100)

And Allah said: "Allah was pleased with the believers when they gave allegiance (*bay'ah*) to you under the tree…" (Fatḥ 48:18)

And Allah said: "Among the believers are men who have proven true to what they pledged to Allah.[1] Some of them have fulfilled their pledge with their lives, others are waiting their turn. They have never changed their commitment in the least." (Aḥzāb 33:23)

1301 – Hudhaifah ﷺ relates that the Messenger of Allah ﷺ said: "Follow those after me; Abū Bakr and 'Umar." (Tirmidhī 3804)

1302 – The Prophet ﷺ said: "My Companions are like stars. Whichever of them you follow, you will be guided." (Abū Ya'lā 2762)

1303 – Anas ﷺ said that the Messenger of Allah ﷺ said: "The likeness of my Companions is like salt in food; food is not good without it." (Abū Ya'lā 2762)

سُوقِهِۦ يُعْجِبُ ٱلزُّرَّاعَ لِيَغِيظَ بِهِمُ ٱلْكُفَّارَ ۗ وَعَدَ ٱللَّهُ ٱلَّذِينَ ءَامَنُوا۟ وَعَمِلُوا۟ ٱلصَّـٰلِحَـٰتِ مِنْهُم مَّغْفِرَةً وَأَجْرًا عَظِيمًۢا ﴿٢٩﴾﴾ [الفتح: ٢٩].
وقال: ﴿وَٱلسَّـٰبِقُونَ ٱلْأَوَّلُونَ مِنَ ٱلْمُهَـٰجِرِينَ وَٱلْأَنصَارِ وَٱلَّذِينَ ٱتَّبَعُوهُم بِإِحْسَـٰنٍ رَّضِىَ ٱللَّهُ عَنْهُمْ وَرَضُوا۟ عَنْهُ وَأَعَدَّ لَهُمْ جَنَّـٰتٍ تَجْرِى تَحْتَهَا ٱلْأَنْهَـٰرُ خَـٰلِدِينَ فِيهَآ أَبَدًا ۚ ذَٰلِكَ ٱلْفَوْزُ ٱلْعَظِيمُ ﴿١٠٠﴾﴾ [التوبة: ١٠٠]. وقال [تعالىٰ]: ﴿۞ لَّقَدْ رَضِىَ ٱللَّهُ عَنِ ٱلْمُؤْمِنِينَ إِذْ يُبَايِعُونَكَ تَحْتَ ٱلشَّجَرَةِ﴾ [الفتح: ١٨]. وقال: ﴿رِجَالٌ صَدَقُوا۟ مَا عَـٰهَدُوا۟ ٱللَّهَ عَلَيْهِ ۖ فَمِنْهُم مَّن قَضَىٰ نَحْبَهُۥ وَمِنْهُم مَّن يَنتَظِرُ ۖ وَمَا بَدَّلُوا۟ تَبْدِيلًا ﴿٢٣﴾﴾ [الأحزاب: ٢٣].

١٢٣١- حدثنا القاضي أَبو عليّ، حدثنا أبو الحُسَيْن، وأبو الفَضْل؛ قالا: حدثنا أَبو يَعْلىٰ، حدثنا أبو عليّ السِّنْجِيّ، حدثنا محمد بن محبوب، حدثنا التِّرْمذي، حدثنا الحَسَن بن الصبَّاح، حدثنا سُفْيان بن عُيَيْنة، عن زائدة، عَنْ عَبْد الملك بن عُمَيْر، عن رِبْعيّ بن (١٢٥/أ) حِرَاش، عن حُذَيفة، قال: قال رسولُ الله ﷺ: **«اقْتَدُوا باللَّذَيْنِ مِنْ بعدي: أبي بكر، وعُمَر»**.

١٣٠٢- وقال: **«أصحابي كالنُّجوم بأيِّهم اقْتَديتُم اهتديتُم»**.

١٣٠٣- وعن أَنس [رَضِيَ اللَّهُ عَنْهُ] قال: قال رسولُ الله ﷺ: **«مَثَلُ أَصحابي كمَثَلِ المِلْحِ في الطعام؛ ولا يصلحُ الطعامُ إلا به»**.

١٣٠٤- وقال: **«اللهَ اللهَ في أصحابي ؛ لا تتَّخذوهم غَرَضاً بعدي ؛**

1304 – The Prophet ﷺ said: "Fear Allah! Fear Allah regarding my Companions! Do not make them targets after me! Whoever loves them, loves them because of his love for me. And whoever hates them, hates them because of his hatred for me. Whoever harms them harms me, and whoever harms me harms Allah, and whoever harms Allah might be suddenly seized."

1305 – The Prophet ﷺ said: "Do not curse my Companions, because if any of you were to donate in charity the weight of Mount Uḥud in gold, that would not equal one *mudd*[9] of theirs, or half a *mudd*." (Bukhārī 3673)

1306 – The Prophet ﷺ said: "Anyone who curses my Companions has the curse of Allah on him, and that of the angels and all people. Allah will not accept any of his obligatory or optional deeds from him." (Suyūṭī's Jāmiʿ Saghīr 8734)

1307 – The Prophet ﷺ said: "When my Companions are mentioned [negatively], hold back." (Haythamī's Majmaʿ al-Zawā'id 7/202)

1308 – The Prophet ﷺ said in the hadith of Jābir رضي الله عنه: "Allah chose my Companions over everything else in existence except for the prophets and the messengers. He specifically chose four of them for me: Abū Bakr, ʿUmar, ʿUthmān, and ʿAlī. He made them my absolute best Companions, and all of my Companions are good." (Bazzār 2763)

1309 – The Prophet ﷺ said: "Whoever loves ʿUmar loves me. Whoever hates ʿUmar hates me." (Ṭabarānī's Awsaṭ via Abū Saʿīd al-Khudhri رضي الله عنه)

1310 – Imam Mālik ibn Anas رحمه الله and others, said: "Whoever hates the Companions and curses them does not have any right to Muslim [war] booty. This ruling is taken from the *āyah*: 'Those who come

9 Translator's Note: One *mudd* = 796 grams

فمن أَحبَّهم فبحبّي أحبّهم، ومن أَبْغَضهم فبِبُغضِي أَبْغَضَهم، ومن آذاهم فقد آذاني، ومن آذاني فقد آذىٰ اللّٰهَ، ومَنْ آذىٰ اللّٰهَ يوشكُ أَنْ يَأْخذَه».

١٣٠٥- وقال: «لا تَسُبُّوا أصحابي ؛ فلو أَنفق أَحدُكم مِثْلَ أُحُدٍ ذهباً ما بلغ مُدَّ أَحَدِهم ولا نَصِيفَه».

١٣٠٦- وقال: «مَنْ سبَّ أصحابي فعليه لَعْنَةُ اللّٰهِ والملائكةِ والناسِ أجمعين، لا يقبلُ اللّٰهُ منه صَرْفاً ولا عَدْلاً».

١٣٠٧- وقال: «إذا ذُكر أصحابي فأَمْسِكُوا».

١٣٠٨- وقال في حديث جابر: «إنَّ اللّٰهَ اختارَ أَصحابي علىٰ جميع العالَمين سِوَىٰ النبيّين والمرسلين، واخْتَار لي منهم أربعةً: أبا بكر، وعُمر، وعُثمان، وعليّاً[٨١] ؛ فجعلهم خَيْرَ أصحابي، وفي أصحابي كلِّهم خير».

١٣٠٩- وقال: «مَنْ أَحبَّ عُمَرَ فقد أحبَّني، ومَنْ أبغضَ عُمَرَ فقد أبغضني».

١٣١٠- [و] قال مالك بن أَنس، وغَيْرُه: مَنْ أَبْغَضَ الصحابةَ وسبَّهم فليس له في فَيْءِ[٨٢] المسلمين حقٌّ، وَنُزِعَ[٨٣] بآية الحشر: ﴿وَمَآ أَفَآءَ

(٨١) في الأصل: «... واختار منهم أربعة: علي وعمر وعثمان وأبي بكر» والمثبت من المطبوع.

(٨٢) (الفيءُ): الغنيمة تؤخذ دون قتال.

(٨٣) (نُزِع): بعد عن الفيء فلا حقَّ له فيه/ قاله الملاّ علي القاري في شرح الشفا ٣/٤٢٦.

after them say, "Our Lord, forgive us and our brothers who preceded us in belief, and do not put rancour into our hearts against those who believe.""" (Ḥashr 59:6-10)

1311 – Imam Mālik said: "Whoever is angry with any of the Companions of Muhammad ﷺ is a disbeliever (*kāfir*) because Allah said: 'He enrages the disbelievers through them (i.e. through the Companions).'" (Fatḥ 48:29)

1312 – 'Abdullāh ibn al-Mubārak said: "Whoever has these two qualities will attain salvation: truthfulness and love for the Companions of Muhammad."

1313 – Ayyūb al-Sakhtiyānī said: "Whoever loves Abū Bakr has established the *dīn*. Whoever loves 'Umar has made the way clear. Whoever loves 'Uthmān has been illuminated by the light of Allah. Whoever loves 'Alī has taken hold of the firm handhold. Whoever praises the Companions of Muhammad a is free from hypocrisy. Whoever disparages any of them is an innovator (*mubtadi'*) who is opposing the Sunnah and the Pious Predecessors (Salaf al-Ṣāliḥ). It is feared that none of his actions will be raised up to heaven until he loves them all and his heart is clean [regarding them]."

1314 – Khālid ibn Sa'īd relates that the Prophet a said: "O people, I am pleased with Abū Bakr so let that be known! O people, I am pleased with 'Umar, 'Alī, 'Uthmān. Ṭalḥah, Zubayr, Sa'd, Sa'īd, and 'Abd al-Raḥmān ibn 'Awf, so let that be known! O people, Allah has forgiven the veterans of Badr and Hudaybiyyah. O people, protect me regarding my Companions and my relations by marriage (i.e. his daughter's husbands). Do not let any of them have cause to demand restitution from any of you for an injustice against them. A wrongful claim will not be granted tomorrow on the Day of Judgement." (Ṭabarānī and Majma' al-Zawā'id 9/157)

ٱللَّهُ عَلَىٰ رَسُولِهِۦ مِنۡهُمۡ فَمَآ أَوۡجَفۡتُمۡ عَلَيۡهِ مِنۡ خَيۡلٖ وَلَا رِكَابٖ وَلَٰكِنَّ ٱللَّهَ يُسَلِّطُ رُسُلَهُۥ عَلَىٰ مَن يَشَآءُۚ وَٱللَّهُ عَلَىٰ كُلِّ شَيۡءٖ قَدِيرٞ ٦ مَّآ أَفَآءَ ٱللَّهُ عَلَىٰ رَسُولِهِۦ مِنۡ أَهۡلِ ٱلۡقُرَىٰ فَلِلَّهِ وَلِلرَّسُولِ وَلِذِي ٱلۡقُرۡبَىٰ وَٱلۡيَتَٰمَىٰ وَٱلۡمَسَٰكِينِ وَٱبۡنِ ٱلسَّبِيلِ كَيۡ لَا يَكُونَ دُولَةَۢ بَيۡنَ ٱلۡأَغۡنِيَآءِ مِنكُمۡۚ وَمَآ ءَاتَىٰكُمُ ٱلرَّسُولُ فَخُذُوهُ وَمَا نَهَىٰكُمۡ عَنۡهُ فَٱنتَهُواْۚ وَٱتَّقُواْ ٱللَّهَۖ إِنَّ ٱللَّهَ شَدِيدُ ٱلۡعِقَابِ ٧﴾ إلى قوله تعالى: ﴿وَٱلَّذِينَ جَآءُو مِنۢ بَعۡدِهِمۡ يَقُولُونَ رَبَّنَا ٱغۡفِرۡ لَنَا وَلِإِخۡوَٰنِنَا ٱلَّذِينَ سَبَقُونَا بِٱلۡإِيمَٰنِ وَلَا تَجۡعَلۡ فِي قُلُوبِنَا غِلّٗا لِّلَّذِينَ ءَامَنُواْ رَبَّنَآ إِنَّكَ رَءُوفٞ رَّحِيمٌ ١٠﴾ [الحشر: ٦ - ١٠].

١٣١١- وقال: مَنْ غاظه أصحابُ محمدٍ فهو كافر؛ قال الله تعالىٰ: ﴿لِيَغِيظَ بِهِمُ ٱلۡكُفَّارَۗ﴾ [الفتح: ٢٩].

١٣١٢- وقال عبدُ الله بن المُبَارك: خَصْلتان مَنْ كانَتَا فيه نجا: الصدقُ، وحُبّ أصحَابِ محمد [ﷺ].

١٣١٣- وقال أيوب السَّخْتِيَاني: مَنْ أَحب أبا بكر فقد أقام الدِّين، ومَنْ أحبَّ عُمر فقد أَوْضَحَ السبيلَ، ومَنْ أحبَّ عثمان فقد اسْتَضَاء بنورِ الله، ومَنْ أحبَّ علياً فقد أخذ بالعُرْوة الوُثْقىٰ، ومَنْ أَحسنَ الثناءَ علىٰ أصحابِ محمد - ﷺ - فقد برئ من النِّفاق، ومن انْتَقَصَ منهم أَحَداً فهو مُبْتَدِعٌ مخالف السُّنَّة[٨٤] والسلف الصالح؛ وأخافُ ألاَّ يَصْعَد له

(٨٤) في المطبوع: «للسنة».

1315 – Someone asked al-Mu'āfā ibn 'Imrān ؓ: "Where does 'Umar ibn 'Abd al-'Azīz rank in relation to Mu'āwiyah ؓ? " He got angry and said: "No one can compare to the Companions of the Prophet a! Mu'āwiyah ؓ was his companion, his relation by marriage [i.e. the brother of his wife, Umm Habiba], his scribe, and someone who was entrusted with the revelation of Allah!"

1316 – A man's funeral bier (*janāzah*) came to the Prophet ﷺ but he did not pray over him, saying: "He used to hate 'Uthmān ؓ, so Allah hates him." (Tirmidhī 3709)

1317 – The Prophet ﷺ said about the Anṣār: "Overlook their faults and mention their good qualities." (Bukhārī 3799)

1318 – The Prophet ﷺ said: "Protect me regarding my Companions and my relations by marriage. Anyone who protects me regarding them will be protected by Allah in this world and the next. And anyone who does not protect me regarding them will be abandoned by Allah, and anyone who is abandoned by Allah might be seized suddenly." (Ṭabarānī and Haythamī's Majma' al-Zawā'id 10/16)

1319 – The Prophet ﷺ said: "Whoever protects me regarding my Companions, I will be his guardian on the Day of Judgment." (Manāhil 1037)

1320 – The Prophet ﷺ said: "Whoever protects me regarding my Companions will be allowed to come to me at the Watering Pool (*Hawḍ*). Whoever does not protect me regarding my Companions will not be allowed to come to me at the *Hawḍ* and will not be able to see me except from a great distance." (Ṭabarānī and Haythamī's Majma' al-Zawā'id 10/17)

1321 – Imam Mālik ibn Anas ؓ said: "This is the Prophet ﷺ; he taught all people *adab;* He a is the one Allah used to guide us to Him; and he a is the one Allah made a mercy for the world (*raḥmatan li*

عملٌ إلىٰ السماء حتى يحبّهم جميعاً، ويكون قَلْبُه سليماً.

١٣١٤- وفي حديث خالد بن (١٢٥/ب) سعيد أَنَّ النبيّ ﷺ قال: **«يا أَيُّها الناس! إني راضٍ عن أَبي بكر فاعْرِفُوا له ذلك. أَيها النَّاسُ! إني راضٍ عن عُمر، وعن عليّ، وعن عثمان، وطلحَة، والزُّبير، وسَعدٍ، وسعيدٍ، وعبد الرحمن بن عَوْف ؛ وأبي عبيدة؛**[٨٥] **فاعرفوا لهم ذلك. أَيُّها الناسُ! إنَّ اللهَ غفَر لأَهلِ بَدْرٍ والْحُدَيْبيَة. أيها الناس! احفظوني في أَصحابي وَأَصْهاري وأَخْتاني، لا يطالبنَّكم أَحدٌ منهم بمَظْلَمَةٍ، فإنها مَظْلَمةٌ لا توهَب في القيامةِ غداً»**[٨٦].

١٣١٥- وقال رجلٌ للمُعَافَىٰ بن عمرانَ: أين[٨٧] عُمر بن عبد العزيز مِنْ معاوية؟ فغضب وقال: لا يُقاسُ بأصحاب النبيِّ ﷺ أَحدٌ، معاوية صاحبُه وصِهْره، وكاتِبُه وأَمينُه عَلَى وَحْي الله.

١٣١٦- وأُتِي النبيُّ ﷺ بجِنَازَةِ رَجُلٍ فلم يُصَلِّ عليه، وقال: **«كَان يُبْغِض عُثمانَ، فأَبْغَضَه الله»**.

١٣١٧- وقال عليه السلام في الأنصار: **«اعْفُوا عن مُسِيئهم، واقْبَلُوا من مُحسِنهم»**.

---

(٨٥) قوله: «وأبي عبيدة»، لم يرد في المطبوع.

(٨٦) أخرجه الطبراني من حديث سهل بن يوسف بن سهل، عن أبيه، عن جده. قال الهيثمي في المجمع ١٥٧/٩: «وفيه جماعة لم أعرفهم». (أختاني): أي أزواج بناته ﷺ.
(مَظْلَمَة): أي ظُلامة. وهي ما يُؤخذ ظلماً وجوراً.

(٨٧) تحرفت في الأصل إلىٰ: «بن».

al-'ālamīn). He ﷺ would venture outside in the darkness of the night to al-Baqī' and make *du'ā* for the people in the graves (i.e. his Companions), asking forgiveness for them the way someone does when seeing his loved ones off on a journey. That is what Allah commanded him to do, and in turn, the Prophet a commanded us to have love and fondness for them and to oppose anyone who opposes them."

1322 – It is related from Ka'b al-Aḥbār ؓ: "There is not a single Companion of Muhammad ﷺ except that he will be allowed to intercede (*shafā'ah*) on the Day of Judgement."[10]

And Ka'b ؓ asked al-Mughīrah ibn Nawfal ؓ to intercede for him on the Day of Judgement.

1324 – Sahl ibn 'Abdullāh al-Tustarī ؒ said: "A person does not truly believe in the Messenger ﷺ if he does not respect his Companions or hold his commands in the highest regard."

10 Translator's Note: Ibn Sa'd narrated this with the wording: "Not a single believer from the family of Muhammad..." (Manāhil 1041)

١٣١٨- وقال: «احْفَظُوني في أصحابي وأَصْهَاري ؛ فإنه مَنْ حفظني فيهم حَفظَه اللهُ في الدنيا والآخرة، ومَنْ لم يحفَظْني فيهم تخلَّىٰ اللهُ منه، ومَنْ تخلَّىٰ اللهُ منه يوشِكُ أن يأخذه».

١٣١٩- وقال عليه السلام: «مَنْ حَفِظني في أصحابي كنتُ له حَافظاً يوم القيامة».

١٣٢٠- و[قال]: «مَنْ حَفِظني في أَصحابي وردَ عَلَيَّ الحوضَ، ومَنْ لم يَحْفظني في أصْحابي لَم يَرِدْ عليّ الحوضَ، ولم يَرَني إلاَّ مِنْ بَعِيد».

١٣٢١- وقال مالك - رحمه الله -: هذا النبيُّ مؤدِّب الْخَلْق الذي هدَانا اللهُ به، وجعله رحمةً للعالمين، يخرجُ في جَوْفِ الليل إلىٰ البَقِيع فَيَدْعُوا لهم ويستغفِرُ كالمُوَدِّع لهم؛ وبذلك أمره الله، وأُمِر النبيّ بحبّهم، ومُوَالاتهم، ومُعاداة مَنْ عَادَاهم.

١٣٢٢- وروى عن كعب: ليس أَحدٌ مِنْ أصْحابِ محمد ﷺ إلاَّ ولَهُ شفاعةٌ يوم القيامة.

١٣٢٣- وطَلَبَ من المُغيرة بن نَوْفَل أَنْ يشْفَع له يوم القيامة.

١٣٢٤- قال سَهْل بن عبد الله التُّسْتَرِيُّ: لم يُؤْمِن بالرسولِ مَنْ لم يُوَقِّرْ أَصحابَه، ولم يُعِزَّ أَوَامره.

Section Seven

The Respect Held by the Prophet ﷺ for His Possessions, for His Locality in Mecca and Medina, and for the Places He Visited or are Well-Known Because of Him

Part of respect and veneration for the Prophet ﷺ is respect for everything connected to him a, respecting the places in Mecca and Medina, and respecting anywhere else the Prophet ﷺ even touched or that is known because of him ﷺ.

1325 – It is related that Safiyyah bint Najdah said: "[A Sahabī named] Abū Madhura had a lock of hair at the front of his head which was so long that it touched the ground when he sat down. He was asked: 'Why don't you cut it off?' He said: 'I will not be the one to cut it off considering that the Messenger of Allah ﷺ touched with his blessed hand."

1326 – Khālid ibn al-Walīd had some hairs from the hair of the Prophet a in his cap (*qulunsuwah*). During one of his battles, his cap fell off and he fought for it in such a fierce and aggressive manner that the Companions of the Prophet ﷺ rebuked him for it due to the great number of men who were killed in the fighting. But he said: "I did not do it for the cap itself, but because of the hair of the Prophet ﷺ that was in it, so that I would not lose its blessing (*barakah*) and to avoid it falling into the hands of the idol-worshippers (*mushrikīn*)."

فصل

ومن إعظامه وإكْبارِهِ إعظامُ جميعِ أَسبَابِهِ، وإكرامُ مشاهِدِه وأَمكنتهِ من مكة والمدينة، وَمَعَاهِدِه، وما لَمَسَهُ عليه السلام أو عُرِف به

١٣٢٥- ورُوِي عن صَفِيّةَ بنت نَجْدَةَ؛ قالت: كان لأَبي مَحْذورَة قُصَّةٌ في مُقَدَّم رأسه، إذا قَعَد وأرسلها أَصابت الأَرضَ. فَقيل له: أَلاَ تحلقُها؟ فقال: لم أَكُنْ بالذي أَحلِقُها، وقد مَسَّها رسُولُ الله ﷺ بِيَدِه.

١٣٢٦- و كانت في قَلَنْسُوة خالد بن الوليدِ شَعَراتٌ من شَعْر رسول الله ﷺ، فسقطتْ قلنسوتُه في بَعْضِ حُروبه، فشدَّ عليها شَدّةً أَنكر عليه أَصحابُ النبيّ ﷺ كَثْرَةَ مَنْ قُتِل فيها؛ فقال: لم أَفعَلْها بسبب القَلَنْسُوة؛ بل لِمَا تضمَّنَتْه من شعْرِه - عليه السلام - لئلا أُسْلَب بركتهَا وتقع في أيدي المشركين.

١٣٢٧- ورُئي ابْنُ عُمر واضعاً يَدَهُ على مَقْعَدِ النبيّ ﷺ من المِنْبَر، ثم وضعها على وَجْهه(٨٨).

---

(٨٨) رواه ابن سعد/ المناهل (١٠٤٤). وسيأتي برقم (١٤٧٨). (مقعد النبي ﷺ): أي مكان قعوده ﷺ.

1327 – Ibn ʿUmar ﷺ was seen placing his hand onto the Prophet's seat on the pulpit (*minbar*) and then placing it on his face. (Ibn Saʿd's Manāhil 1044)

1328 – That was the reason why Imam Mālik ﷺ did not ride an animal in Medina. He used to say: "I have too much modesty (*ḥayā'*) before Allah to trample with an animal's hoof on the land where the Messenger of Allah ﷺ is buried."

1329 – It has been narrated that Imam Mālik ﷺ gave many horses that he owned to Imam al-Shāfiʿī ﷺ as a gift, and Imam al-Shāfiʿī said to him: "Keep one of them with you." So Imam Mālik replied to him with an answer similar to the previous answer [i.e. #1328].

1330 – Abū ʿAbd al-Raḥmān al-Sulamī ﷺ related that Aḥmad ibn Faḍlawayh – the ascetic (*zāhid*) who was a mighty archer and raider – said: "I never touched a bow with my hand except when I am in a state of purity (*ṭahārah*) since I heard that the Prophet ﷺ held a bow with his hand."

1331 – Imam Mālik ﷺ issued a verdict (fatwa) about someone who said: "The soil of Medina is bad" that he should be given 30 lashes and then imprisoned. The man had some standing in society (and people felt the fatwa was overly strict), but Imam Mālik said: "How urgently he needs to have his head cut off! The soil in which is buried the best of human beings – the Prophet ﷺ – and he claims that it is not good!"

1332 – The Ṣaḥīḥ states that the Prophet ﷺ said about Medina: "Whoever innovates something in it, or gives shelter to an innovator in it, has the curse of Allah, the angels, and all people on him. Allah will not accept his obligatory or optional deeds from him." (Bukhārī 1870)

١٣٢٨- ولهذا كان مالك - رحِمَه الله - لا يركبُ بالمدينة دابّةً؛ وكانَ يقول: أَسْتَحِي من الله أَنْ أَطَأَ تُرْبةً فيها رسولُ الله بحافِرِ دابّة.

١٣٢٩- ورُوي [عنه] أنه وهب للشّافعي كُراعاً[٨٩] كثيراً كان عنده؛ فقال له الشافعيُّ: أَمْسِك منها دابّةً. فأجابه بمثل هذا الجواب.

١٣٣٠- وقد حكىٰ أبو عبد الرحمن السُّلَمي عن أحمد بن فَضْلَوَيه الزَّاهد - وكان من الغُزاة الرُّماة - أنه قال: ما مَسَسْتُ القَوْسَ بيدي إلاّ علىٰ طَهارة منذ بلغني أَنَّ النبيَّ ﷺ أخذ القوسَ بيده.

١٣٣١- وقد أَفْتىٰ مالكٌ فيمن قال: تربةُ المدينة رَدِيّةٌ[٩٠] - يُضْرَبُ ثلاثين دِرّةً[٩١]، وأمر بحَبْسه، وكان له قَدْرٌ، وقال: ما أَحْوَجه إلىٰ ضَرْبِ عُنُقه! تُربةٌ دُفِنَ فيها خير البشر: النبيُّ ﷺ، يزعمُ أنها غير طيبة!!

١٣٣٢- وفي الصحيح أنه قال عليه السلام - في المدينة: «**مَنْ أحدث فيها حَدَثاً أو آوىٰ مُحْدِثاً فعليه لَعْنَةُ اللهِ والملائكةِ والناسِ أجمعين؛ لا يقبلُ اللهُ منه صَرْفاً ولا عَدْلاً**».

١٣٣٣- وحُكي أن جَهْجَاهاً الغِفَاريَّ أَخَذَ قضيبَ النبيِّ ﷺ من يد عثمان [رضي اللهُ عنه] وتناوله لِيكْسِره علىٰ رُكْبته، فصاح به الناسُ، فأخذته الآكِلَةُ في رُكبته فقطعها، ومات قبل الحَوْلِ.

---

(٨٩) الكُراع: اسم لجميع الخيل/ النهاية.

(٩٠) رديّة: فاسدة.

(٩١) دِرَّة: السوط يضرب به/ المعجم الوسيط.

1333 – It is related that on one occasion Jahjah al-Ghifārī took the staff of the Prophet ﷺ from the hand of 'Uthmān ﷺ and tried to break it across his knee, so people began shouting at him to stop. Suddenly, gangrene (*ukāl*) appeared on his knee which led to it being amputated, and he died before the end of the year.

1334 – The Prophet ﷺ said: "Whoever swears an oath on my pulpit (*minbar*) while he is lying, let him prepare to take his seat in the Fire." (Abū Dāwūd 3246)

1335 – And I narrate that when Abū al-Faḍl al-Jawharī ﷺ came to Medina to visit and he drew near to its houses, he dismounted his conveyance and began walking and weeping, reciting the following poetry:

When we saw the traces (i.e. the places) left by the Chosen One ﷺ

who did not bequeath us a heart or intellect capable of fully recognizing the value of his traces,

We alighted from our saddles to walk out of respect for him ﷺ,

because it is clear that riders should dismount for him ﷺ.

1336 – It is related that when a certain visitor looked onto the city of the Messenger of Allah ﷺ, he began to recite the poetry:

The veil is lifted from us and a moon shines out to those who look on, banishing all illusions.

When our mounts reach Muhammad ﷺ, it is forbidden for us to be found on our saddles.

We are drawing near to the best man ever to walk on the earth,

so we hold this ground in the highest of respect and honour.

١٣٣٤- وقال عليه السلام: «مَنْ حلف على مِنبري كاذِباً فَلْيَتَبَوَّأْ مَقْعَدَهُ من النَّارِ».

١٣٣٥- وحُدِّثْتُ أنَّ أبا الفضل (١٢٦/ب) الجَوْهري لما وردَ المدينةَ زائراً، وقَرُب من بيوتها تَرَجَّلَ ومشى باكياً، يُنشِد(٩٢):

وَلَمَّا رَأَيْنا رَسْـمَ(٩٣) مَنْ لَمْ يَدَعْ لنَا فُؤَاداً لِعرْفانِ الرُّسومِ ولا لُبّا(٩٤)

نَزَلْنَا عَنِ الأَكْوَارِ(٩٥) نَـمْشِي كَرَامَةً لِمَنْ بانَ(٩٦) عَنْهُ أَنْ نُلِـمَّ به رَكْبا(٩٧)

١٣٣٦- وحُكى عن بعض المُرِيدين أنه لما أَشرف على مدينة الرسول صلى الله عليه وسلم أنشد يقول متمثِّلاً:

رُفِع الـحِجَابُ لنا فَلَاحَ لناظرٍ قَمَرٌ تَقَطَّعُ دونَهُ الأَوْهَامُ

وإذا المَطِيُّ(٩٨) بنا بَلَغْنَ مُـحَمَّدًا فَظُهورُهُنَّ على الرِّجَالِ حَرَامُ

قَرَّبْنَنَا مِنْ خَيْرِ مَنْ وَطِيءَ الثَّرَىٰ ولـها عَلَيْنَا حُرْمَةٌ وذِمَامُ(٩٩)

---

(٩٢) في المطبوع «مُنشداً». والبيتان من قصيدة للمتنبي في مدح سيف الدولة الحمداني.

(٩٣) رسم: المراد به آثار المصطفى ﷺ في معاهده ومساكنه.

(٩٤) لعرفان: لمعرفة. (لُبّا): اللُّبُّ: العقل الخالص من الشوائب.

(٩٥) الأكوار: جمع كُوْر: وهو للإبل بمنزلة السَّرج للفرس.

(٩٦) بان: ظهر رَسْمُهُ/ قاله القاري.

(٩٧) أن نُلمّ به رَكْبا: أي لا يليق بنا – وقد قرب مقام الحبيب – أن نأتيه راكبين.

(٩٨) المَطِيُّ: جمع مَطِيَّةٍ، وهي الناقة التي يركبُ مَطاها: أي ظهرها/ النهاية.

(٩٩) ذمام: أي حقٌّ وحرمة. والأبيات لأبي نواس في مدح محمد الأمين العباسي.

1337 – It is related that one of the sheikhs went on Hajj by foot and when asked why he did that, to which he said: "[Does] the runaway slave come back to the home of his master while mounted?! If I had been able to walk on my head, I would not have walked on my feet!"

1338 – Qāḍī 'Iyāḍ ﵀ comments on this, saying: "This level of respect is befitting for the places where revelation descended; where Jibrīl and Mīkā'īl ﵉ frequently visited; where the angels and the *Rūḥ* (Jibrīl ﵇) descended; where the sounds of worship and glorification of God rang out; the place whose soil contains the body of the Master of Humanity ﷺ; and from which the *dīn* of Allah and the Sunnah of His Messenger spread.

One must respect the places where the *āyāt* of the Qur'an were studied; the masjids in which the salat was performed; the places that witnessed great virtue and tremendous good deeds; the places which saw great nobility and graciousness was shown; the places which saw undeniable miracles and proofs; the places associated with the religious rites of the *dīn*; the sacred places of the Muslims; the places where major events occurred regarding the master of the Messengers ﷺ; the places where the Seal of the Prophets lived (Allah bless and give peace to him and his entire family) from which prophecy poured forth and where its waves flowed; the places which witnessed the message of Allah; and the first piece of land that the skin of the Prophet ﷺ touched after his passing. Its fragrance should be inhaled, and its residences and its walls should be kissed.

The poet said:

O Abode of the Best of the Messengers ﷺ, and the one by whom

people were guided, who was chosen to receive the āyāt.

For you I have intense love, tender love, and yearning which kindles the very embers of my heart.

١٣٣٧- وحُكي عن بعض المشايخ أنه حجَّ ماشياً؛ فقيل له في ذلك؛ فقال: العَبْدُ الآبِقُ(١٠٠) لا يأتي إلىٰ بيت مولاه راكباً، لو قدرتُ أنْ أَمشِيَ علىٰ رأسي ما مشيتُ علىٰ قَدَمَيَّ.

١٣٣٨- قال القاضي: وجدير لِمَوَاطنَ عُمِّرت بالوَحْيِ والتنزيل، وتردَّدَ بها جبريلُ وميكائيل، وعرجَت منها الملائكة والرُّوحُ، وضَجّت عَرَصَاتُها بالتقديس والتسبيح، واشتملت تُرْبَتُهَا علىٰ جَسدِ سيّدِ البَشَر، وانتشر عنها مِنْ دين الله وسنّةِ رسوله ﷺ ما انتشر، مدارسُ آياتٍ(١٠١)، ومساجدُ صلواتٍ(١٠٢)، ومشاهِدُ الفضائلِ والخيرات، ومعاهدُ البراهين والمعجزات، ومَنَاسِكُ الدِّين، ومشاعِرُ المسلمين، ومواقفُ سيد المرسلين، وَمُتَبَوَّأ(١٠٣) خاتمِ النبيّين - ﷺ وعلىٰ عترته أجمعين - حيث انفجرت النبوَّة، وأين فاضَ عُبَابُها(١٠٤)، ومَوَاطن مَهْبِط الرسالة؛ وأول أَرضٍ مَسَّ جِلْدَ المصطفىٰ تُرَابُها، أَنْ تُعَظَّم عَرَصاتُها، وتُتَنَسَّم نفحاتها، وتُقَبَّل رُبوعها وجُدْرَانها(١٠٥):

---

(١٠٠) الآبق: الهارب.

(١٠١) مدارسُ آيات: محال يدرس فيها القرآن.

(١٠٢) في المطبوع: «ومساجدُ وصلوات». (المساجد): مواضع السجود. (الصلوات): جمع صلاة، وهي العبادة المعروفة.

(١٠٣) متبَوَّأ: أي منزل.

(١٠٤) العبابُ: كثرة الماء والسيل.

(١٠٥) في الأصل زيادة: «شعر».

I have a vow: if I ever fill my eyes with those walls and the places where you walked.

There, my beturbaned grey hair will be covered with dust from so much kissing.

Had it not been for obstacles and foes, I would always visit them, even if I had to be dragged away by my feet.

But I will be guided in my eagerness to greet the inhabitants of those houses and rooms.

By a scent purer than the purest musk which covers him each morning and evening.

He is gifted with pure blessings and increased in them through prayers for peace and blessings on him!

يا دارَ خَيْرِ المُرْسَلِينَ ومَنْ بِهِ هُدِيَ الأَنامُ وخُصَّ بالآياتِ

عِنْدي لأَجْلِكَ لَوْعَةٌ(١٠٦) وصَبابَةٌ(١٠٧) وَتَشَوُّقٌ مُتَوَقِّدُ الـجَمَرَاتِ

وعَلَيَّ عَـهْدٌ إنْ مَلأْتُ مَـحاجِرِي(١٠٨) مِنْ تِلْكُمُ الْـجُدْرَانِ والعَرَصاتِ

لأُعَفِّرَنَّ(١٠٩) مَصُونَ شَيْبِي بَيْنَـها مِنْ كَثْرَةِ التَّقْبيلِ والرَّشَفَاتِ

لولا العَوَادِي(١١٠)، والأعَادِي زُرْتُـها أَبَدًا ولو سَـحْباً عَلَىٰ الوَجَناتِ

لٰكِنْ سَأُهْدِي مِنْ حَفيلِ(١١١) تَـحِيَّتِي لِقَطِينِ(١١٢) تِلْكَ الدَّارِ والـحُجُراتِ

أَزْكىٰ من الـمِسْكِ المُفَتّقِ(١١٣) نَفْحةً تَغْشَاهُ بالآصالِ والبُكُراتِ

وَتَـخُصُّهُ بِزَواكِيَ الصَّلواتِ ونوامِيَ التَّسْلِيْـمِ والبَرَكَاتِ

---

(١٠٦) اللوعة: حرقة في القلب وألم يجده الإنسان من حبٍّ أو نحوه.

(١٠٧) الصَّبابة: رِقَّةُ الشوق وحرارته.

(١٠٨) محاجري: المحْجرُ في العين: ما أحاط بها.

(١٠٩) لأعفِّرنَّ: لأُمرِّغنَّ.

(١١٠) العوادي: العوائق.

(١١١) الحفيل: الكثير النفيس.

(١١٢) لِقطين: أي المقيم.

(١١٣) المفتَّق: ما خلط بغيره ليزداد طيباً.

www.ingramcontent.com/pod-product-compliance
Lightning Source LLC
Chambersburg PA
CBHW020949090426
42736CB00010B/1333
* 9 7 8 1 9 5 2 3 0 6 4 7 1 *